Traversing the Darkness

A Spiritual Journey

Written By James Miller

Copyright

Traversing the Darkness

Disclaimer

This book is intended for **educational and informational purposes only**. It reflects the author's personal experiences, perspectives, and independent inquiry, and is not a substitute for professional medical, psychological, psychiatric, legal, or financial advice.

The concepts discussed, including nervous-system regulation, trauma-related patterns, communication dynamics, and the Mirror-Linguistic Hypothesis, are presented as a framework for reflection and exploration. They are not presented as clinical diagnoses, treatment protocols, or guarantees of outcome. Readers should not use this book to self-diagnose, to discontinue or modify prescribed treatment, or to delay seeking professional help.

If you are experiencing mental health distress, persistent anxiety or depression, intrusive thoughts, trauma symptoms, suicidal ideation, or any condition that affects your safety or daily functioning, please seek support from a qualified healthcare professional. If you believe you may be at immediate risk of harm to yourself or others, contact emergency services or your local crisis support provider right away.

Any references to research, theory, or physiology are included to support discussion and should be interpreted within the limits of this book's scope. The author is not providing medical or clinical services, and no professional relationship is created by reading this book.

To the fullest extent permitted by law, the author and publisher disclaim liability for any loss, injury, or damage arising from the use of or reliance upon the information in this book. You are solely responsible for how you interpret and apply the material.

Contents

Preface

There are some journeys a person chooses, and others that seem to arrive uninvited.

This book was not written because I believed I had mastered life, or because I wanted to present myself as someone who had found all the answers. It was written because, over time, I came to realise that much of what I had lived through was never fully understood while I was inside it. Some of it felt like confusion. Some of it felt like a loss. Some of it felt like frustration that had nowhere to go. Some of it felt like silence, the kind that does not always bring peace but arrives when words no longer feel safe or when being heard feels uncertain.

For much of my life, I carried experiences I could feel but could not fully explain. I knew what it was to feel misunderstood. I knew what it was to feel something deeply, but not have the language, support, or emotional environment to make sense of it. I knew what it was to speak and feel that what I meant had not landed. I knew what it was to go quiet, not because nothing was happening inside me, but because too much was happening at once. Those patterns did not begin in adulthood. They were there early. They stayed with me. In different ways, they shaped how I related to myself, to others, and to the world around me.

Looking back, I can now see that many of the moments I once dismissed, or simply endured, left deeper impressions than I understood at the time. Small scenes became lasting imprints. A family gathering. A false accusation. The feeling of trying to express something honestly and not being believed. The internal tension that followed. The emotional charge that stayed in the body long after the moment had passed. When you are young, you do not always know how to name those things. You only know that something in you has changed.

This book is, in many ways, an attempt to honour that truth.

It is not simply a record of pain, though pain is part of it. It is not only about trauma, conflict, relationships, conditioning, or awakening, though all of those live somewhere within these pages. More than anything, this is a book about learning to face what once felt too heavy, too confusing, or too hidden to meet directly. It is about what happens when the darkness is no longer treated as something to outrun, but something to walk through carefully, truthfully, and with as much presence as possible.

The word *spiritual* can mean many things to many people. For me, it is not about performance, image, superiority, or pretending to exist above ordinary human struggle. It is not about abandoning the body, or denying pain, or claiming certainty where there is still mystery. It is about becoming honest enough to listen inwardly. It is about noticing what is happening beneath the surface. It is about recognising when the life you are living no longer fits the deeper truth that is trying to emerge. It is about learning to trust what is real, even when doing so changes your relationships, your direction, and your sense of self.

My journey did not unfold in a straight line. It was marked by confusion, anger, collapse, withdrawal, grief, learning, and reflection. It involved looking back at childhood with different eyes. It involved recognising patterns I had once normalised. It involved seeing how the body holds what the mind cannot always organise. It involved accepting that some of my strongest reactions were not signs of weakness or failure, but signs that something deeper needed understanding. Over time, that realisation changed the way I saw my past, my pain, and my place in the world.

I have not written this book to place myself above anyone. I have written it because I know what it is to live with inner tension that others do not fully see. I know what it is to search for language for experiences that seem to sit somewhere between emotion, memory, instinct, and spirit. I know what it is to slowly piece together a life from fragments that once felt disconnected. And I know, too, that many people carry private darkness while appearing functional on the surface.

So this book is offered in that spirit.

Not as a sermon.
Not as a performance.
Not as a final answer.

But as an honest account of moving through shadow, learning from it, and discovering that some forms of darkness do not arrive to destroy us, but to reveal what we can no longer afford to ignore.

If any part of these pages helps you feel less alone in your own journey, more trusting of your inner life, or more willing to face what you have spent years avoiding, then this book will have done something worthwhile.

James Miller

Introduction

There comes a point in some lives when what once held everything together no longer works.

The routines still exist. The responsibilities remain. The world carries on. From the outside, things may even look fairly normal. But inwardly, something begins to shift.

The old explanations start to lose their grip. The identities that once felt familiar begin to feel strained.

The ways of coping that once seemed necessary no longer provide relief. What was once manageable becomes heavy.

What was once hidden begins to rise. And somewhere in the middle of that process, a person may begin to realise that they are not simply going through a difficult period. They are being asked to meet themselves more honestly than ever before.

This book is about that meeting.

Traversing the Darkness is not a book about perfection, nor is it a neat story of falling apart and then emerging fully healed. It is a book about the difficult, often unglamorous process of facing what lives beneath the surface of a life.

It is about emotional pain, childhood imprinting, misunderstanding, silence, grief, identity, relational wounds, nervous system strain, spiritual awakening, and the long, uneven process of integration. It is about what happens when you stop trying to outrun your own depth.

The darkness spoken of in this book is not only external. It is not just the darkness of events, losses, conflict, or betrayal. It is also the darkness of inner disconnection. The parts of us we do not understand.

The emotions we were not taught how to hold. The truths we learned to suppress to belong, survive, or keep the peace. The stories we inherited without choosing.

The ways we adapted long before we understood what we were adapting to. Sometimes darkness is suffering. Sometimes it is confusion. Sometimes it is numbness. Sometimes it is the ache of knowing something is wrong long before you can explain why.

For me, the journey through darkness involved recognising that many of my responses had roots deeper than the present moment. It involved seeing that what appeared, on the surface, as anger, silence, shutdown, overthinking, sensitivity, withdrawal, or inner chaos often had a history.

It involved realising that the body remembers what the conscious mind cannot always organise neatly. It involved understanding that emotional pain is not always irrational just because it is difficult to explain.

It involved seeing that some of the deepest struggles in life come not from being weak, but from being shaped by experiences that were never properly understood, supported, or resolved.

At the same time, this is not a book that stays only with pain. It is also about awakening.

By awakening, I do not mean adopting a spiritual identity, escaping reality, or claiming special insight. I mean something more grounded than that. I mean, becoming able to see.

To see patterns. To see inherited dynamics. To see how old wounds continue to echo through present relationships. To see when your body is reacting before your mind can make sense of it.

To see where you have abandoned yourself, where you have silenced yourself, where you have accepted too little, and where you have mistaken survival for peace. Awakening, as I have lived it, is less about becoming someone new and more about returning to what was buried beneath fear, confusion, and adaptation.

This book is written for those who have felt things deeply but struggled to explain them.

For those who have questioned themselves because others could not understand their experience.

For those who have lived through inner conflict while trying to keep functioning outwardly.

For those who have mistaken silence for peace, people-pleasing for love, and endurance for healing.

For those who have sensed that their pain carried meaning, even before they had language for it.

It is also written for those who are willing to look back without becoming trapped there. Because reflection matters, but so does movement. Understanding matters, but so does integration. This book does not ask the reader to stay inside old wounds. It asks something gentler and more demanding: to look honestly, to feel truthfully, and to begin relating to oneself with more clarity, responsibility, and compassion.

The pages that follow move through memory, fracture, conditioning, emotional inheritance, identity, breakdown, awakening, and return. Some chapters are intimate and personal.

Others widen into reflection. But the thread running through all of them is the same: that healing does not begin when life becomes easy. It begins when we stop abandoning what is real inside us.

That is what this journey has taught me.

Darkness is not always the end of sight.
Sometimes it is the place where deeper sight begins.

Part I - The Fracture

Some wounds do not begin with one great collapse, but with smaller moments that quietly split the world in two.

A look that changes.
A tone that hardens.
A truth that is spoken, but not received.
A feeling that rises, but has nowhere safe to go.

Part I is about those moments.

It is about the early fractures that form before we understand what we are carrying. Before we have the language to explain ourselves. Before we know how to distinguish between being emotional and being overwhelmed, between being sensitive and being unsafe, between being difficult and being misunderstood.

This is the territory where the first cracks begin to appear, not always as dramatic events, but as repeated experiences that slowly shape the nervous system, the personality, and the private relationship a person has with their own inner world.

For me, this part of the journey begins with a feeling I came to know long before I could name it properly: the feeling of trying to express something real and not being met.

Not being believed. Not being understood. Not being seen in the way I knew, even as a child, that I was trying to be seen. Some of those moments were small on the surface, but they did not land small inside me.

They stayed. They echoed. They taught my body things my mind could not yet organise.

They taught me that expression did not always lead to connection. That speaking up could lead to tension. That silence could become a form of protection.

This section is not written to assign blame, nor to flatten the complexity of childhood into a list of injuries. Childhood is rarely that simple. Love and pain can exist in the same home. Care and confusion can come from the same people. Moments of warmth can live beside moments of rupture.

What matters here is not creating villains.

What matters is telling the truth about impact. It is possible to have been loved and still left struggling. It is possible to have been cared for and still misunderstood.

It is possible to have grown up around people doing their best, and still carry wounds they did not know they were leaving behind.

The fracture, then, is not one thing. It is a series of internal divisions.

It is the split between what was felt and what was acknowledged.

The split between who I was and who I learned to be.

The split between my outer behaviour and the inner experience driving it.

The split between my need to speak and my growing instinct to go quiet.

The split between the version of me others reacted to and the version of me I knew myself to be.

Those divisions do not stay in childhood. They travel. They show up in school, where systems reward certain kinds of expression and quietly suppress others. They show up in families, where silence can mean peace one day and punishment the next.

They show up in identity, where self-protection slowly becomes personality. They show up in relationships, where old misunderstandings return wearing new faces. And, for a long time, they can show up in the body before they ever become conscious thought.

That is why this part matters.

Before there can be awakening, there has to be honesty.
Before there can be integration, there has to be recognition.
Before there can be peace, there has to be a willingness to look at where the first inner tensions began.

The chapters that follow trace those early imprints.

They move through memory, school, family, and the quiet adaptations that helped me survive but slowly pulled me away from myself.

They are not presented as abstract theory, but as lived terrain. This is the ground beneath the rest of the book. These pages hold the early atmosphere of my life: the confusion, the sensitivity, the tension, the silence, the longing to be understood, and the first signs that something deeper was happening beneath what others could see.

If the latter parts of this book are about walking through darkness with greater awareness, then this part is about recognising where the dimming first began.

It begins before the language.
Before the explanations.
Before the frameworks.
Before the spiritual awakening had a name.

It begins where many journeys begin, though not everyone realises it at the time:

with a child trying to be heard, and learning far too early that being honest does not always mean being received.

Chapter 1 - Before I Had Words

Some of the deepest moments in a life do not arrive with explanation. They arrive as feeling.

Before there is language, there is atmosphere. Before there is understanding, there is sensation. Before a child can organise an experience into something neat and tellable, the body has already begun to register what safety feels like, what tension feels like, what warmth feels like, and what it means to be suddenly cut off from belonging.

When I look back now, one of the clearest early moments I can still feel did not begin as some dramatic event. It happened at a family gathering, around a large table, in the main living room, while everyone was singing Happy Birthday. The room was a little dim. I remember the light. I remember the faces around me. But more than anything, I remember looking toward my nonno and singing. I was there. I was involved. I was doing my part. And then, in what felt like an instant, I was told I had not been singing at all.

That moment has stayed with me for years, not because of the song itself, but because of what happened inside me when I was not believed.

The first feeling was not calm disappointment. It was much quicker and much deeper than that. There was hurt in it, and disbelief, and confusion, but what came through most explosively was anger. It happened fast, before I had the ability to stand outside myself and assess it. My reaction did not unfold in a neat, conscious sequence. It erupted. I can see now that the anger came before I had words for what was happening. Before I could explain myself properly. Before I could slow anything down. At that age, I had no framework for nervous-system reactions, no understanding of pre-conscious activation, no concept of how quickly a child can move from connection into rupture. I only knew that I was trying to participate, and suddenly I was being told that what I knew I had done had not happened.

What upset me most was not simply the accusation. It was not believed.

That distinction matters.

Children can recover from misunderstandings surprisingly quickly when they feel seen, when someone pauses, softens, and checks what really happened. But something different occurs when a child knows they are telling the truth and discovers that truth alone is not enough. Something internal shifts.

It is not only the event itself that leaves a mark, but the experience of realising that your sincerity may still fail to reach the people around you. Even then, I think some part of me felt the injustice of it. Not in an adult, philosophical way. Not as a fully formed thought. But as a shock to the system. A young body recognising that expression does not guarantee recognition.

That moment did not stay confined to the party. It carried on.

I remember the week after as draining, tense, and deeply upsetting. The emotional charge did not simply pass through me and leave. It stayed in my body as pressure, unease, anxiety, and depletion. At that age, I could not have named nervous-system collapse, but when I reflect now, that is what it felt like.

I held onto the truth of what had happened, but the situation around me narrowed until the only thing that seemed to matter was my reaction.

I was pushed to apologise, and eventually I did, because I wanted things to settle.

But apologising when you still feel that the original truth has not been acknowledged leaves a strange kind of residue. It creates a conflict inside.

On one level, you take accountability for the outburst.

On the other hand, you are left holding the pain of knowing no one took accountability for wrongly blaming you in the first place.

That combination is hard enough for an adult to process. For a child, it is bewildering.

Looking back, I do not think what stayed with me was just the incident. It was the lesson it quietly taught.

It taught me that speaking up could become complicated.
It taught me that being visible was not always safe.
It taught me that I could be present, sincere, and engaged, and

still be told I had failed to show up.

Perhaps most painfully, it taught me that once a reaction becomes the focus, the cause of that reaction can disappear from everyone else's view.

There is a difference between being loud and being heard. I did not know that then, but I felt it.

As I grew older, that early pattern did not vanish. It echoed.

I often found that when I tried to express myself, especially around certain people, I felt an edge in the air before anything had even been said.

Tension did not always arrive through direct words. Sometimes it lived in the atmosphere, in body language, in the feeling of being dismissed before I had finished speaking. Around one family member in particular, I always felt on edge.

There was an unspoken tension, and disagreement was often met with hostility, disbelief, or frustration. It took me a long time to understand how much repeated experiences like that shape a person.

Not only psychologically, but physically. How the body learns to anticipate dismissal.

How expression begins to carry risk. How the nervous system starts reading differences as something unsafe to bring forward.

This is one of the difficulties with early emotional memory: the body often understands before the mind can follow.

A child may not say, "I feel relationally unsafe," or "my system is bracing against invalidation." A child simply feels the pressure. The heat. The collapse. The tightening. The inability to find words. Over time, those responses begin to organise behaviour. For me, one of those behaviours was silence.

When I went silent, it was not because nothing was happening inside me. It was because too much was happening.

Silence was not emptiness. It was a controlled withdrawal. A form of protection. I remember tension, unease, a feeling of energy moving through my body with nowhere to go. In that state, speaking did not feel like access. It felt blocked.

What I can see now is that silence sometimes became the only available way to keep from being flooded further.

It gave shape to something that otherwise felt overwhelming. And yes, people treated me differently when I was quiet than when I was expressive.

Quietness was often easier for others to tolerate. Expression demanded that something be met. Silence demanded less from those around me, even when it cost more inside me.

That pattern did not exist only in one moment. It was reinforced by the emotional atmosphere around me as I was growing up.

There were times when my father lost control emotionally, and though I understand much more now about the pain he was carrying, the child in me still felt what happened in those moments. I remember one incident around a Christmas gift that did not work. I had done nothing to it, but I was accused of breaking it.

I did not explode then in the same way I had at the birthday party. I remember standing still. I remember crying.

I remember hearing words I could not simply unhear. Comments that reduced me, compared me, made me feel smaller than I already felt.

In those moments, the body braces in ways memory does not always capture neatly.

You freeze. You watch. You absorb. The experience does not always stay as a story. Sometimes it stays as a tone in the nervous system.

I want to be careful here, because this is not a chapter about condemning my family. It is about telling the truth of impact.

There was love in my upbringing.

There was care. There were good moments, real moments, warm moments.

But warmth does not erase rupture, and love does not automatically produce understanding.

A child can be loved and still left struggling to make sense of experiences that were too charged, too inconsistent, or too unprocessed by the adults around them.

That is one of the hardest truths to hold with maturity: that people can love you deeply and still wound you in ways they do not fully see.

When I try to describe what being misunderstood feels like in the body, it is hard to reduce it to one sensation. At different times, it has felt like heat, pressure, shutdown, numbness, anger, sadness, disbelief, confusion, and emotional dissonance all layered together. It can feel like wanting to move towards someone and retreating at the same time.

It can feel like an internal protest with no clear outlet. It can feel like trying to hold onto the truth of your own experience while the room around you quietly reorganises itself against it.

Those are strong words, but they are the closest I can come to describing something I have lived many times.

Misunderstanding is not always a minor social inconvenience. Sometimes it lands like a fracture in one's basic trust that reality can be shared honestly with others.

I think that is why this memory matters so much.

It was not only about being told I had not sung. It was about something more foundational.

It was about the beginning of a question that would follow me for years: what happens to a person when they keep trying to meet the world sincerely, but repeatedly feel that the world is not meeting them back in kind?

For a long time, I did not have the language for that question.

I did not know how much of my later life would be shaped by it.

I did not know how often I would feel that same old tension in different rooms, different relationships, different conversations.

I did not know how often I would find myself caught between wanting to express what I felt and wanting to disappear into quiet because quiet felt safer than dismissal.

But the roots were there early. Not fully formed. Not fully understood. Just present. Waiting.

If I could reduce the voice of that younger self to one sentence, it would be this:

You refuse to believe me, see me, or hear me, and it is not because I did not try. I always did my part. But it seems many could not meet me where I was.

That sentence holds more than childhood pain. It holds the beginning of the fracture.

Not because I was broken beyond repair, but because something in me had begun to divide.

One part still wants to speak.

Another learning cost.

One part still trusting sincerity.

Another learning is that sincerity might not be enough.

One part reaching outward. Another pulling inward for safety.

That is where this journey begins.

Not with a grand revelation.
Not with a spiritual insight.

But with a child who was present, who was trying, and who discovered far too early how lonely it can feel when truth does not land.

Perhaps that is where many deeper journeys begin:

not in certainty, but in the ache of having once been there fully, and still not been received.

Chapter 2 - The Invisible Curriculum

There is what the school says it is teaching, and then there is what it teaches without ever naming it.

On paper, school is meant to educate. It is meant to develop the mind, widen possibilities, and prepare a person for life.

But alongside lessons, tests, subjects, and qualifications, there is often another curriculum running quietly underneath it all.

A curriculum made not only of information, but of tone, timing, hierarchy, permission, pressure, approval, dismissal, and adaptation. It is there in the way a child learns when to speak and when to stay quiet.

It is there in what kinds of questions are welcomed and what kinds are brushed aside.

It is there that children are seen as promising, who are seen as troublesome, and who are slowly taught to edit themselves just to move through the day without friction.

I did not have that language when I was young. I could not have said I was being shaped by an invisible curriculum. But I felt its effects.

One of the earliest signs was simple enough on the surface:

I did not want to go to school. I was very young, and I did not have a clear explanation for why.

I only knew there was something in me that resisted it. At that age, people tend to want reasons that sound reasonable, neat, and easy to respond to.

But not every child can explain a feeling in a way adults are prepared to hear. Sometimes the feeling arrives long before the words.

Sometimes all a child knows is that something does not sit right, that the environment feels wrong in ways they cannot articulate, or that being placed within a certain setting awakens a distress they do not know how to organise.

That was closer to my experience.

I did not have a problem with every teacher or every classmate. I just did not want to go, and I could not explain why.

In time, I was taken in, spoken to, and brought back into the system. On the outside, that might sound like the issue was resolved. But what often gets missed in these moments is that compliance is not the same as understanding.

A child can return to routine while still carrying confusion in their body. They can appear to settle while still learning that emotional discomfort must be pushed past, not explored.

They can continue attending while absorbing a quieter lesson: that's what they feel is less important than whether they can function. That lesson leaves a mark.

School taught me many things, but it taught me very little about my own value.

What it made much clearer was the relationship between approval and performance. Grades, qualifications, achievement, discipline, acceptable behaviour, measurable progress, these were the currencies that made sense within the system.

To do well was to be validated.

To struggle was to risk being misread.

To move at a different pace, react differently, need more processing time, or experience things more intensely was not often met with curiosity.

More often, it was interpreted through behaviour. And behaviour, in institutional settings, is rarely understood in depth. It is managed.

There were parts of school I genuinely enjoyed. I do not want to flatten the experience into something wholly negative, because that would not be true.

I found many subjects interesting. I was intellectually stimulated at times. I received praise. I earned certificates. I did well in subjects I enjoyed, and when I later moved into environments where independent study suited me better, my performance improved significantly.

College, especially, showed me that I was more capable than some earlier experiences had led me to believe.

That mattered. It gave me a form of confidence that school itself had not always been able to offer consistently. But the existence of good experiences does not cancel out the deeper pattern. The deeper pattern was that I often felt emotionally misunderstood inside systems that were more equipped to measure output than interpret distress.

That misunderstanding could show up in small but lasting ways.

I remember being singled out on occasions when my actions were not intentional in the way they were perceived.

A teacher once picked me out for being rude or disruptive when, in reality, I had simply been distracted by the same atmosphere as others around me.

But I was the one sent out. It is difficult to explain how much these moments can imprint on a child, especially when they already carry sensitivity, confusion, or a sense of being slightly out of step with their environment. What stays is not always the exact wording. Often, it is the energy of the exchange. The voice.

The facial expression. The feeling of being selected as the problem. The internalisation that someone dislikes you, or has decided who you are, and that nothing you say in that moment will shift it.

Even years later, I could still remember the feeling of that teacher's approach more clearly than the specific language used.

That is part of the invisible curriculum, too: the body learns from tone as much as from content.

A child quickly begins to notice which adults feel safe, which feel dismissive, which are fair, and which carry a charge that puts them on edge before a lesson even begins.

For me, some teachers were encouraging, thoughtful, and clearly cared. I remember one in particular standing out because of his authenticity. Someone asked him who he was voting for, and he calmly refused to answer, explaining that he had to remain impartial as a teacher.

That stayed with me because it felt clean. It felt principled. It felt like a man aware of the power of influence, choosing not to misuse it.

Moments like that mattered because they showed me that authority did not always have to become control.

There could be integrity within the role.

There could be care without intrusion.

There could be education without imprinting.

But other messages were less explicit and far more formative.

Most of the time, emotional expression in school was not really welcomed in any deep sense. The message was usually to calm down, be quiet, pay attention, and carry on.

Distress was not something to sit with. It was something to get past. If someone was visibly dysregulated, overwhelmed, frustrated, or unable to process what was happening, the focus usually fell on the disruption, not the cause. There was little room for exploring what lived underneath.

That kind of environment teaches children to separate inner reality from outer acceptability.

It teaches them to present calm, or at least controllability, even when something in them is not calm at all.

It teaches them that fitting the rhythm of the room matters more than understanding their own rhythm.

I think this is where a subtle form of self-division deepens.

The child starts learning not only subjects, but also social survival. They notice which qualities gain approval and which provoke irritation. They see who is liked. They observe how certain people carry themselves. Around the age of ten or eleven,

I can remember becoming more aware of this in a quiet way.

I noticed someone who was well-liked, and I found myself observing how they stood, how they moved, how they presented themselves.

I do not think I was consciously inventing a false identity, but I can see now that some form of masking began to reveal itself there.

Not as deliberate deception. More as an adaptation.

A picking up of signals. A refining of outward presentation in response to what seemed to work socially.

This is one of the more hidden effects of school:

Children do not only learn what to know, they learn what to seem like.

Yet, for me, the tension was never straightforward.

I did not feel like I was always performing in a calculated way.

In many respects, I was simply myself. I could mix with different kinds of people. I could move between groups.

I did not consciously set out to invent a character to survive the day. But even without deliberate performance, there were still adaptations taking place.

There were moments where I minimised myself. Moments where I stopped speaking up because it seemed to unsettle others. Moments where I held back, not because I had nothing to say, but because I could feel how quickly confidence in one person could become resentment in another.

At times, I found that if I knew an answer, contributed enthusiastically, or showed pride in part of my background, it could irritate people rather than invite connection.

So, as many children do, I learned to adjust. Not all at once. Not dramatically. Just enough to reduce friction.

That is another hidden lesson of school:

Authenticity is often encouraged in theory, but selectively tolerated in practice.

Children are told to think for themselves, but not always in ways that disturb the structure.

They are told to be creative, but not so creatively that they move outside what can be easily managed.

They are told to participate, but not in ways that challenge the emotional comfort of the room.

They are told to grow, but often within already approved boundaries.

I do not say that to dismiss every teacher or every educational experience. Rather, I say it because systems tend to have limits, and children feel those limits in their bodies long before they can analyse them intellectually. I did. Even when I could not have explained it, I could feel the difference between genuine encouragement and conditional acceptance. Between being seen and being managed. Between being taught and being shaped.

There is also a quieter grief in this chapter, which is that some of my strengths only became clearer once I was in environments that suited me better.

Later on, through independent study, college, and more self-directed learning, I found that I could focus deeply, perform well, and thrive when the atmosphere allowed for it. I was praised for dedication. I received awards. Lecturers recognised my ability.

That does not simply prove that I was capable. It also reveals something about the mismatch that existed earlier.

A child can carry an ability that is partly obscured by the environment. They can have intelligence that does not show up cleanly under pressure, intimidation, emotional neglect, or repeated misreading. They can begin to doubt themselves, not because they lack something essential, but because the conditions around them are not bringing their best into view.

That recognition came later. At the time, all I had were fragments.

A sense that some teachers did not like me.
A sense that emotional reality was inconvenient in a classroom.
A sense that certain people could not separate my behaviour from their judgement of me.
A sense that my inner life was far more complex than the labels placed on it.
A sense that I was being asked, in subtle ways, to comply with rhythms and expectations that did not always match what was happening inside me.

None of this made me reject learning. If anything, it made me value real learning more. But it did make me wary of systems that confuse obedience with understanding, or order with care.

When I think now about what the invisible curriculum really was, I would put it this way: it was the education of my nervous system inside an environment that did not always know it was teaching me.

It taught me how quickly the atmosphere affects the body. It taught me that authority can soothe or destabilise. It taught me that misunderstanding can become internalised if repeated often enough. It taught me that children do not only learn through lessons, but through the emotional conditions in which those lessons are delivered.

It taught me that part of my journey would involve disentangling real intelligence from the ways I had once felt diminished, misread, or pressured to become more manageable than truthful.

By the time I left school, I had gained more than knowledge of subjects. I had also absorbed patterns of silence, adjustment, and observation that would continue to shape me long after the classroom had gone. Some of those patterns were useful. Some became burdens. Some would take years to understand properly.

But that is how the fracture deepens.

Not always through one great harm.
Sometimes through repetition.
Through small dismissals.
Through atmospheres that go unnamed.
Through being bright in one context and diminished in another.
Through learning, little by little, that surviving a system may require a person to drift further from the simple truth of how they actually feel.

When that happens early enough, the child may not even know there is another way.

Chapter 3 - My Parents Were Once Children Too

It takes time to realise that the people who raised you were not only parents. They were also shaped beings. Carrying histories. Carrying wounds. Carrying loyalties, fears, habits, and emotional patterns that had begun long before you arrived.

As a child, it is difficult to see. Children do not usually meet their parents as complex human beings first. They meet them in the atmosphere. As tone. As regulation or dysregulation. Comfort, absence, unpredictability, reassurance, tension, warmth, silence, anger, touch, distance.

The child does not begin with a biography. The child begins with impact. Only later, if reflection deepens and resentment softens enough to let understanding in, do the parents begin to come into view as people who were themselves shaped by worlds they did not fully choose.

My father's childhood was not simple. He grew up in a family marked by discipline, movement, and harshness.

My grandfather had been in the military, and the family moved often because of those postings. Discipline was not abstract in that world; it had force behind it. My father was hit often and not treated well at times.

That matters, not because it excuses everything, but because it gives context to a man I would later know as both loving and emotionally volatile, at times hard to connect with, and at other times deeply caring. When I was younger, I could feel the instability before I could understand its roots. Later, I came to recognise that some of what I had experienced in him was not random anger appearing out of nowhere, but a nervous system carrying old injury, still reacting from places much older than the present moment.

My mother came from a different cultural and emotional atmosphere, but not an uncomplicated one. She was raised in an Italian family that, in some ways, felt closer and more connected.

There was more family time, more togetherness, less open arguments in certain respects. But closeness is not the same as emotional attunement, and warmth in one area does not prevent neglect in another.

The head of that family, my nonno, could be strict, and at times, what I now understand as narcissistic. My mother was not always given the support or attention she needed. She was often dismissed in favour of other siblings.

That left its own imprint. It showed me that pain does not always arrive through obvious brutality.

Sometimes it arrives through being overlooked, through uneven attention, through hierarchy inside the home, through the quiet message that your emotional reality holds less weight than someone else's.

When I look back now, I can see that both of my parents were carrying something unfinished.

My father carried emotional turmoil from how he had been raised.

My mother carried patterns of withdrawal and dismissal that had roots in her own history. Neither of them, in my view, was intentionally cruel.

That distinction matters to me. I do not write this chapter from a place of wanting to punish them on the page.

I write it from a place of wanting to tell the truth about inheritance.

The truth is that we do not only inherit eye colour, temperament, and surnames.

We inherit atmospheres.

We inherit coping styles.

We inherit what people have normalised.

We inherit what they have never learned to name, and unless something interrupts those patterns, they continue moving. Not always identically, but recognisably.

There were times when my father would lose control emotionally, and as a child, it could feel as though it had appeared without warning.

Later, I understood it differently. I saw more clearly that what once felt like eruptions "for no reason" were often triggered states in a nervous system that had been shaped by repeated early pain.

That understanding did not erase the effect on me, but it changed the emotional frame around it.

It helped me move from simple resentment toward a more difficult and more mature truth: sometimes the people who unsettle us most are acting from parts of themselves that were never properly settled to begin with.

My mother's pattern, when distressed, was often different. If she became upset or angry, she could withdraw completely and ignore me for hours. For a child already struggling to make sense of emotional tension, that kind of absence can be deeply destabilising.

A raised voice is one kind of rupture; silence is another. In some ways, silence can be harder to process because it offers so little to work with.

There is no explanation to respond to, no clear shape to push against, only absence, delay, emotional distance, and the child's own escalating confusion.

I know now that this, too, came from pain and from not knowing how to respond differently in those moments. But at the time, it left me with questions I could not answer.

It taught me to live around unspoken things. It taught me how much uncertainty can be created when a child feels the emotional weather changing but is given no map for it.

This is part of what I mean by emotional inheritance.

Children do not only learn from what parents say. They learn from what parents cannot say.

They learn from how tension is carried through the house. They learn from how quickly a mood can change.

They learn whether conflict can be repaired or whether it must simply be waited out.

They learn whether emotional pain can be spoken, or whether it becomes shouting, coldness, silence, comparison, shutdown, or displacement onto somebody smaller.

They learn these things before they realise they are learning them.

There were unspoken rules in my home. One of them was that when tension was high, silence was often safer than expression.

I was told, at times, that children should be seen and not heard.

That phrase may sound small to some ears, but phrases like that do not land as theory in a child.

They land as shaping forces.

They become part of the emotional architecture of the home.

They help teach when voice is welcome and when it is inconvenient. Over time, they can turn a person inward, not always because they have nothing to say, but because the environment has trained them to associate expression with friction.

And yet, alongside all of this, there was real love.

That is what makes chapters like this difficult to write honestly. It would be easier, in some ways, if the story were one note.

If there had only been harm, this chapter could be cleaner. But that would not be true.

There were many moments of warmth, real safety, and genuine care with my parents. Birthdays often felt authentic and celebratory.

There were times of tactile affection, hugs, closeness, shared life, support, and encouragement. My parents helped me financially.

They backed me in practical ways. They wanted the best for me, even when they did not know how to deal with me emotionally.

I believe that deeply. I do not doubt their love.

What I have had to come to terms with is that love and wounding can coexist. People can love you and still leave confusion in you. They can want good for you and still pass on patterns they never healed in themselves.

That is where compassion becomes more difficult and more meaningful.

Compassion without truth becomes denial.
Truth without compassion becomes hardness.
I have tried, over time, to hold both.

There were years when I could not make sense of how I felt so different from my parents in certain moments.

At times, I accepted who they were and how they were.

At other times, I could not fathom how we were even related.

But the older I became, the more I saw them not only as the people who affected me, but as people affected by others before them.

I began to understand more about what they had carried. In later years, I even felt, in some respects, that I was parenting them emotionally through my own growing self-awareness.

Not in a controlling sense, but in the sense that I had begun doing the inner work needed to understand them and myself better, and that changed the emotional field between us.

I also came to see how much of their relationship dynamic had been absorbed into me.

The moods. The anger. The frustration. The silence. The sudden shifts between warmth and coldness.

The tendency, under strain, either to explode or to go completely quiet. For a long time, those patterns felt imprinted in me. I could see both parents in parts of my own temperament, especially when I was unstable, and that can be a painful recognition. There is grief in realising that some of what troubles you most in yourself is not entirely self-created. But there is also freedom in that recognition, because what is inherited can be seen, and what is seen can begin to change.

There were broader family tensions, too, and they carried emotional weight.

I remember a period when my grandparents fell out with my parents over something as seemingly ordinary as invitations to a party, and the fracture lasted for nearly two years. It affected me more than I understood at the time.

As I became more aware of how my father had been treated, I did not want to be around them.

Then, when those relationships later began to repair, I still went long periods without seeing them. Distance had become easier than involvement. Looking back, that too was part of the legacy.

Conflict was never just between individuals; it spread across generations, across gatherings, across loyalties, across who saw whom and who didn't. Children notice these absences, even when adults think they are shielding them.

Over time, though, something softened.

My parents did apologise. They made it clear they loved me deeply and had not understood how to deal with me. They acknowledged that they had issues of their own to work through and that they never wanted me to feel unwanted. That mattered to me. It did not rewrite the past, but it opened something. It created room for understanding where only pain might otherwise have remained.

I believe they are proud of me. I believe they always wanted good for me, even if they could not always embody what I needed while I was growing up.

That is part of healing, too: not pretending harm never happened, but allowing later truth to enter the story where it genuinely belongs.

When I ask myself now what I forgive them for, the answer is not theatrical. I forgive them for what they were unaware of.

I forgive them for being part of larger cycles they did not create but carried.

I forgive them for the limits of their own emotional education. I forgive them for not having the language, the tools, or the inner stability that might have changed certain moments.

I do not say that lightly, and I do not say it to sound evolved. I say it because I have lived long enough to understand that many parents are trying to raise children while still carrying injuries from their own childhoods.

Some hide that fact better than others, but the inheritance is there all the same.

If they had lived in a different world, with more healing, less pressure, more emotional support, and more freedom from the strain that life places on people, perhaps some things would have unfolded differently. But even with all that was imperfect, I still see them as great parents in many ways. They were not monsters. They were human beings, doing their best with the awareness they had, shaped by their own histories, passing on both care and confusion, both strength and unfinishedness. That is not a neat story. It is a human one.

That is why this chapter matters.

Because healing does not always begin with blame. Sometimes it begins with seeing more fully.

Seeing that what hurt you may have also hurt them.

Seeing that your parents were not born as "mum" and "dad" but arrived there through lives of their own. Seeing that emotional inheritance is not an abstract concept, but something lived in tones of voice, patterns of absence, habits of reaction, and the atmospheres children grow up inside without ever consenting to them.

I cannot tell the truth of my own spiritual journey without telling this truth too: part of awakening was realising that the people who shaped my earliest world were themselves shaped by darkness they had not fully traversed.

Perhaps one of the quiet tasks of a life is this:

to receive what was passed down,
to recognise it without hatred,
and to decide, with as much honesty as possible,
What will continue through you, and what will end with you?

Chapter 4 - The Lies I Told Myself to Survive

Not every lie begins as deceit. Some lies begin as an adaptation.

They begin in childhood, not because a child wants to betray themselves, but because the self is still forming inside environments that do not always know how to receive it.

A child does not sit down and consciously decide, I will now abandon parts of myself to survive. It happens more quietly than that.

A feeling is dismissed often enough.

A truth is met with resistance often enough.

A need becomes inconvenient often enough. And somewhere along the way, the child begins to make small internal bargains.

If I am easier, maybe I will be loved.
If I am quieter, maybe I will be safer.
If I do more for others, maybe I will matter.
If I stay agreeable, maybe I will not be left.
If I question myself first, maybe their rejection will hurt less.

Those bargains rarely sound so clear at the time. More often, they become atmosphere. Habit. Personality. Identity. They become the quiet lies a person lives with for years before recognising them as lies at all. That dynamic sits at the centre of this chapter, and of so much of what followed in my life: the slow conversion of pain into self-story, and self-story into self-limitation.

One of the deepest beliefs I carried was that I was somehow not enough.

Not good-looking enough.
Not clever enough.
Not socially capable enough.
Not stable enough.
Not valuable enough.

I did not hold these beliefs constantly or consciously every day, but they were there in the background.

They showed up in doubt, in comparison, in the aftertaste of being misunderstood, in the emotional charge left behind by conflict, and in the tendency to interpret difficult experiences as evidence that something must be wrong with me.

When a child grows up feeling repeatedly misread, dismissed, or emotionally unsupported, it is easy for the mind to internalise the wrong conclusion. Instead of seeing that the environment lacked understanding, the child often assumes that the flaw must be within the self.

That is one of the cruellest distortions survival creates. It turns contextual pain into personal verdict.

Looking back now, I can see that I did not have one single survival strategy. I had several.

At times, I was rebellious.

At times compliant.

At times humorous.

At times withdrawn.

At times visible in ways I did not want.

At times invisible in ways I did not choose.

That mixture makes sense to me now.

The body and mind are pragmatic when they are trying to preserve connection, reduce harm, or find a way through emotionally confusing terrain. They do not always settle on one fixed response.

They reach for whatever seems most likely to work in a given moment. What matters is not which strategy was "correct," but the cost of living inside them for too long. Survival may protect something necessary in the short term, but if left unexamined, it can quietly become character.

One of the ways this showed up in me was through over-giving.

I liked helping people. I still do. It brings me genuine satisfaction to contribute where I can, to support, to encourage, to make life a little lighter for someone else if I am able. But over time, I had to confront a more difficult truth:

There were periods where helping crossed over into people-pleasing, and people-pleasing crossed over into self-rejection. I was not always giving from wholeness.

Sometimes I was giving in the hope of maintaining harmony, preserving closeness, or securing a place in the emotional lives of others.

That is a painful thing to recognise, because on the surface it can look like generosity, yet underneath it may carry fear, fear of conflict, fear of disapproval, fear of being unnecessary, fear of being left with one's own unmet needs.

When giving becomes a strategy for safety, it no longer feels clean. It becomes exhausting. It starts to hollow the person who is always extending themselves outward.

There were also many moments when I said I was okay when I was not.

This is one of the more complicated forms of self-betrayal, because it can look so ordinary from the outside. A person continues.

They function. They smile when needed.

They explain away what hurts.

They keep moving.

But inside, something is shutting down. In my own life, there were times when emotional and mental shutdown would build into something much more overwhelming.

The cycle would repeat:

strain, suppression, flooding, collapse. At the time, I did not have the language or clarity I have now. I only knew that I could move from appearing functional to being deeply overwhelmed in ways that others often misread as deliberate bad behaviour rather than what they felt like to me:

automatic responses of a system under too much stress.

That gap between lived experience and how others interpreted it deepened the wound.

It reinforced the sense that even my distress could be turned into evidence against me.

What makes this kind of pain particularly difficult is that it often gets moralised.

People do not always see overwhelm as overwhelm.
They see "too much."
They see "difficult."
They see "dramatic."
They see "nasty."
They see "unreasonable."

Once a person is repeatedly met in that way, it becomes easy to start questioning their own reality, not because they know their pain is false, but because the world around them keeps treating it as inconvenient, exaggerated, or illegitimate.

In my case, I did not lose awareness of my feelings.

What I often lost was confidence that they would ever be understood fairly. That distinction matters. The lie was not always that my pain is not real. The lie was often more subtle than that:

Perhaps I must carry this alone; perhaps I ask too much by wanting it to be seen; perhaps I should blame myself first and question others later.

That is how self-gaslighting can begin, not always through denial of pain, but through repeated relocation of responsibility away from those causing harm and back onto the self who is trying to survive it.

Another important lie sat inside the confusion between attention and love.

There were times in relationships where attention felt like care, where pursuit felt like intimacy, where someone wanting access to me felt, initially, like proof of value. But with time,

I began to recognise how easily attention can become possessiveness, how quickly need can disguise itself as love, and how often guilt and control can enter relationships dressed as closeness.

I had my own part in those dynamics, and I have no interest in presenting myself as blameless.

But I do see more clearly now that some of what I once accepted as connection was actually dependency, emotional confusion, and projection.

When you have grown up trying to maintain closeness through adaptation, it can take years to recognise that being wanted is not the same as being loved well.

There is also grief in realising what it costs to be the "easy" one.

For me, the cost was my own self-identity and self-worth.

That is not a small admission. It means there were periods of life where I had become so oriented towards keeping things calm, managing other people's reactions, avoiding unnecessary conflict, or making excuses for the behaviour of others that I drifted away from a simpler relationship with myself.

I did not lose myself all at once. It happened gradually, in compromises, in silences, in excessive patience, in trying to be understood by those who had little intention of understanding, in giving chance after chance where clarity would have been kinder.

This is how survival can become self-erasure:

not through one dramatic surrender, but through repetition. Through the daily quieting of one's own knowing in order to stay inside the dynamics that should have been questioned much earlier.

Yet, beneath all of that, something in me remained intact.

That part matters.

Because even when I was doubting myself, even when I was making excuses for the behaviour of others, even when I was performing calmness, helpfulness or patience beyond what was healthy, there was still a part of me that knew something was not right.

I may not always have had the words. I may not always have acted on it quickly enough. But I did not fully lose contact with that deeper knowing. I observed. I felt. I noticed. I carried an inner sense that what was happening around me, and at times within me, could not be the whole truth of who I was.

That inner signal would become increasingly important later. It was one of the first threads leading out of confusion and towards awakening.

If I let the inner child in me speak plainly here, without polish, without caution, it would say something close to this:

It was all unnecessary. I did my best. It was not fair to keep making me the scapegoat, to place things on me that were never only mine to carry, to dismiss what I was facing while asking me to accommodate what others refused to face in themselves.

There is pain in that voice, but there is also truth.

and that truth closes Part I.

Because what this first section of the book has really been tracing is not simply childhood memory, family tension, school conditioning, or early misunderstanding in isolation.

It has been tracing the formation of an internal world.

A world in which I learned, slowly and often painfully, how easy it is for the self to split when expression is not received, when adaptation is rewarded more than truth, and when the child begins to construct a workable self out of what is tolerated rather than what is real.

The fracture was never only external. It became internal, too. That is what these chapters have shown.

The wound was not only in what happened. It was what I came to believe about myself because of what happened.

That is why Part II must go where it goes next.

Because once the lies begin to loosen, once performance starts to crack, once self-protection can no longer convincingly pass for peace, a person enters a darker territory.

A more demanding one.

The stage where what was once managed rises more fully into view.

The stage where the body speaks louder, where the inner conflict intensifies, where old patterns repeat in adult life with heavier consequences, and where certainty itself begins to fail.

Part I has shown where the fracture began.

Part II enters what the fracture became.

Part II - The Darkness

There comes a stage in many journeys where the old strategies stop working, but the new self has not yet formed clearly enough to take their place. This is the darkness. Not darkness as theatre. Not darkness as identity. Not darkness as something to romanticise.

But darkness as confrontation. The part of life where what has been buried no longer stays buried. Where the body starts keeping score in ways that can no longer be ignored.

Where old emotional patterns begin showing up in adult relationships, in stress, in silence, in overreaction, in confusion, in withdrawal, in exhaustion, in compulsive attempts to explain, repair, appease, or escape.

This section of the book is slower, heavier, and more introspective for a reason.

It is the point where survival stops feeling like protection and starts feeling like imprisonment. It is the point where the deeper work begins.

If Part I was the fracture, Part II is the descent into what that fracture carried forward.

These chapters move through the body, emotional formation, adult relational patterns, inner conflict, and the collapse of false certainty.

They explore what happens when pain is no longer treated as an isolated incident, but recognised as something that has shaped perception, behaviour, identity, and the private relationship a person has with themselves.

This is not the part of the story where everything becomes clear. It is the part where the clearing begins by forcing what is unresolved into view.

Chapter 5 - The Body as a Biological Witness

This chapter turns towards the body, not as an inconvenience or an enemy, but as a record of emotional history.

It explores how pain, tension, shutdown, agitation, collapse, and looping internal states can live in the body long before the mind fully understands what is happening. It opens the deeper question of what it means to see distress not as moral failure, but as a patterned response.

It is the beginning of learning that the body often tells the truth long before the intellect is ready to admit it.

Chapter 6 - Neurodevelopment and Emotional Formation

This chapter explores the shaping of emotional life more deeply:

What happens when feelings are inconsistently received, when safety is unstable, when language for inner states is limited, and when self-regulation develops under strain rather than support?

It looks at the formation of sensitivity, emotional confusion, numbness, and self-reliance, and it asks how a person learns to interpret their own inner world when so much of it has gone unmirrored.

Chapter 7 - The Shadow Code

Here, the focus shifts more directly into adult repetition: the hidden rules, behavioural patterns, fears, loyalties, and adaptations that carry childhood into later relationships.

This chapter examines overexplaining, abandonment fear, emotional over-responsibility, silence, shutdown, and the tendency to stay too long inside harmful dynamics while trying to prove, fix, endure, or be understood.

It is a chapter about patterns that once felt normal, becoming impossible to ignore.

Chapter 8 - The Myth of the Rational Mind

This chapter enters the conflict between what we know, what we feel, and what we override.

It explores the moments where intuition speaks, but old conditioning stays seated longer than it should.

It looks at cognitive dissonance, emotional reasoning, defended realities, and the painful experience of recognising that facts alone do not resolve relational confusion when fear, projection, and ego are driving the exchange. It is about the breakdown of the comforting fantasy that clear thinking alone can save us from unprocessed pain.

Chapter 9 - Silence, Isolation, and the Void

This chapter brings the section to its deepest still point. It turns towards loneliness, collapse, withdrawal, and the in-between state where the old self no longer fits but the new self has not yet stabilised. It is the chapter of unravelling, but also of listening. Of discovering that the silence once used for protection may become, in another phase of life, the very place where deeper truth starts to gather. It is not yet a resolution, but it is the threshold of it.

Part II matters because this is where the journey stops being theoretical.

This is where the cost becomes visible.
Where the body becomes impossible to dismiss.
Where relationships reveal what the mind had tried to soften.
Where inherited patterns become personal responsibility.
Where pain stops being an atmosphere in the background and becomes something that must be faced directly.

If Part I asked, Where did the fracture begin?
Part II asks something more difficult:

What has that fracture been doing inside me all this time?

Chapter 5 - The Body as a Biological Witness

For a long time, I thought what I was struggling with lived mainly in my mind.

I believed the confusion was something to think my way through.

I believed the pain could be understood if I just found the right explanation, the right perspective, the right language.

At times, I thought that if I could become more rational, more controlled, more disciplined in my thinking, then I would finally be able to settle what had been unsettled in me for so long.

But the deeper truth was that much of what I was experiencing had never been living only in thought. It had been living in my body all along.

That realisation did not arrive all at once. It came slowly, and then suddenly. It came through repetition.

Through recognising patterns I could no longer explain away.

Through moments where my body reacted before my mind had caught up.

Through the growing awareness that some of what I was carrying did not behave like ordinary thought at all.

It behaved like something older, something faster, something more instinctive and automatic than the conscious explanations I kept trying to impose upon it.

When I look back now, I can see that the body had always been involved.

It had been there in the early tension, in the silence, in the emotional charge that stayed long after particular events had ended.

It had been there in the collapse that followed moments of conflict, in the pressure I could not name as a child, in the confusion that seemed too large for the situation in front of me.

Even before I had language for any of it, my body was recording.

Not in words, not in tidy memories, but in sensations, reactions, and patterns of response that would continue to shape me for years.

There is a kind of memory that does not tell a story.

It does not present itself neatly or ask to be understood through logic first. It simply returns as sensation.

A tightening in the chest.

A heat rise. A sudden agitation.

A collapse into numbness.

A sharp internal shift that seems to arrive before thought has had any chance to organise what is happening.

For a long time, those moments puzzled me, because I was still trying to interpret them as if they belonged to the present moment alone.

I thought I was reacting only to what was in front of me. I did not yet understand that the body does not always distinguish between what is happening now and what feels familiar from before.

That is one of the most difficult things to explain to people who have not lived it. From the outside, a reaction can appear excessive, irrational, disproportionate, or sudden.

But from the inside, it rarely feels random.

It feels connected to something, even if that connection cannot yet be spoken.

It feels like the body already knows what the mind is only just beginning to suspect, and because I lacked the language for this for so long, I often turned the problem back on myself. Why am I reacting like this?

Why can't I just let it go?

Why does this affect me so deeply?

Why can I understand something intellectually and still not feel settled by that understanding?

These questions followed me for years, and the mistake within them was subtle but important.

They assumed the body was malfunctioning when in truth it was often responding consistently to what it had learned.

One of the clearest turning points in this recognition came while driving one day.

I remember feeling irritated, frustrated by delays, by the pace of things, by the sense of being held up.

It would have been easy to treat that as ordinary impatience, the kind of reaction people brush off without much thought.

But on that day, something in me paused long enough to ask a different question: Why are you getting angry?

I remember the strangeness of that moment, because the answer did not come cleanly. It was not that I was in some genuine rush or facing some urgent problem.

It was that something was occurring automatically, out of proportion to the circumstances, and for the first time, I recognised it clearly enough to see that it was happening before I had consciously chosen it.

That moment changed a great deal for me. It opened the possibility that processes were unfolding in my body and nervous system that I had been living inside without properly understanding.

Once that door opened, many things began to look different.

I started to see that some of the states I had treated as personal failures were not simply failures of will.

They were accumulated responses. They were patterned reactions.

They were my body doing what it had been conditioned to do under strain, even when, consciously, I would have preferred something else.

That did not remove responsibility from my life, but it changed the kind of responsibility I needed to take. Instead of condemning myself for not being more controlled, I had to begin learning what my body had been carrying, what it had learned to anticipate, and how it had come to react before thought could intervene.

That shift matters because the nervous system does not argue. It does not wait for your most mature explanation.

It does not calmly review your intentions before responding. It reacts.

It protects. It anticipates. It moves quickly, and it does so based on what it has registered as significant, threatening, painful, or unresolved.

For years, I had the strange and often exhausting experience of knowing, on one level, that I was not in danger while feeling, on another level, that my body had not received that message at all.

That contradiction creates a deep internal divide.

You know one thing intellectually, but your body behaves as if something else is true, and unless you understand that split, it is easy to start distrusting yourself.

There were periods in my life where this was especially pronounced.

I could appear functional on the surface and yet be carrying enormous inner strain.

I could be moving through ordinary life while my body was holding tension

I barely noticed anymore because it had become so familiar.

I could feel drained in ways that did not seem explained by physical tiredness alone.

I could shift from coping to shutting down with a speed that felt frightening and confusing, and because these things are often misread by others as temperament, attitude, or choice, the wound deepens.

What is happening in the body gets turned into a judgement on character.

Distress becomes "too much." Overwhelm becomes "bad behaviour."

The collapse of a strained system becomes something moralised, as though the body had failed some test of decency rather than reached a threshold it could no longer absorb.

This is why I have had to revisit my own story with greater care. There were many times in the past when I interpreted my responses through shame first.

I assumed there must be something wrong with me. But over time, I began to ask a different question:

not what is wrong with me, but what has happened to me that my body is still responding to?

That question did not erase the pain, but it did change the emotional atmosphere around it. It replaced some of the self-judgement with curiosity. It opened up the possibility that there was coherence beneath what had once felt chaotic.

It allowed me to consider that my body was not simply getting in the way of my life, but trying to tell the truth of it in the only language it had always known.

I also began to notice how clearly the body responded to safety.

Not just threat, but safety. Some places and experiences calmed me in ways I did not understand at the time.

I would go out walking, spend time in nature, sit quietly in the park, move away from the density of home or the intensity of certain environments, and something in me would begin to settle. I did not fully appreciate then that my body was recognising those spaces as safer than the others.

I was leaving behind. I only knew they helped. Looking back now, I can see that those moments were not accidental comforts. They were my system finding places where it could exhale, places where the tension dropped enough for me to return to myself, even briefly.

That, too, became part of the learning. The body was not only a site of pain. It was also a guide. It was showing me, often long before the mind could explain it, what environments activated me, what interactions unsettled me, what routines dulled my awareness, and what kinds of spaces or rhythms allowed something calmer and more grounded to emerge.

Once I started listening more closely, I could feel how certain environments pushed me into autopilot, how repeated scrolling, repetitive work dynamics, or emotionally charged family settings subtly altered my internal state. I could feel the shift.

I could recognise when my body was becoming more vigilant, more compressed, more alert to the emotional field around me.

With that awareness came a new kind of choice. Not perfect control, but greater participation.

Greater ability to notice what was happening before it swallowed me whole.

This did not mean that everything suddenly became easy.

There were still periods of collapse, hypersensitivity, confusion, and inner intensity.

There were still times when the body moved faster than my conscious understanding. But the relationship had begun to change. I was no longer only trying to override what I felt. I was beginning to listen.

To observe. To ask what my body was telling me rather than immediately trying to silence it. That changed everything, because once the body is no longer treated purely as the problem, it becomes possible to see it as a witness. A biological witness to what has been lived, absorbed, repeated, and carried. A witness not only to pain, but to adaptation, endurance, and the possibility of healing.

In many ways, this chapter marks a deeper descent into the truth of the journey. Part I showed where the fracture began. Here, in Part II, the fracture begins to show itself not only in memory or belief, but in the body itself. In breath. In tension. In shutdown.

In reactivity. In the quiet and often hidden ways, the nervous system keeps a record of what the conscious mind could not yet fully bear or explain.

The darkness is not only emotional or spiritual. It is embodied. It lives in the places where the body has had to carry what the mind could not organise, and where the person I was had to keep moving long before I understood what was moving through me.

That is why this recognition matters so much.

Because healing, for me, did not begin when I learned to think differently in some abstract way. It began when I stopped treating the body as something to conquer and started recognising it as something that had been telling the truth all along. Not the whole truth, not the final truth, but a truth I could no longer afford to ignore.

It had been carrying memory beneath memory, pain beneath explanation, and signals beneath language. And once I began to hear that, the journey changed.

Chapter 6 - Neurodevelopment & Emotional Formation

There is a stage in life where we begin to realise that not everything we feel belongs only to the present moment.

At first, that realisation is subtle. It appears as a question more than an answer.

Why does this affect me so deeply?

Why do certain situations seem to reach further into me than others?

Why do I respond in ways that feel immediate, almost automatic, even when part of me can see what is happening?

For a long time, I tried to understand those experiences through logic alone. I thought that if I could explain them clearly enough, I would gain control over them.

But what I was encountering was not something that had been formed through logic in the first place. It had been formed much earlier, in ways that were quieter, less visible, and far more influential than I had realised.

What I began to understand, slowly, is that emotional life does not start when we become conscious of it.

It begins much earlier, in the environments we grow up in, in the ways we are responded to, in what is mirrored back to us and what is not. It begins with how our nervous system learns to interpret the world before we have the language to question those interpretations.

As a child, I did not sit and analyse my emotional responses.

I lived inside them. If something felt tense,

I felt it. If something felt confusing,

I carried that confusion. If something felt unsafe or unpredictable, my body adapted to that, whether I understood it or not. And those adaptations did not disappear as I grew older.

They became part of how I experienced myself, others, and the world.

There is a difference between feeling something and understanding something.

As a child, I felt a great deal, but I did not always have the support or language to understand what I was feeling.

When a feeling is not understood, it does not simply vanish. It lingers. It shapes how future experiences are interpreted. It becomes part of a pattern.

I can see now how much of my emotional formation was shaped by inconsistency.

There were moments of closeness and warmth, and there were moments of tension, withdrawal, or unpredictability.

There were times when I felt seen, and times when I felt dismissed or misunderstood. There were moments when the connection felt natural, and moments when it felt like something I had to work for, manage, or preserve.

That kind of environment does something subtle but powerful. It teaches the system to stay alert.

Not always in an obvious way. Not always in panic. But in readiness.

In scanning. In a quiet, ongoing attempt to read the room, to anticipate shifts, to sense when things are about to change.

That sensitivity can look like awareness. And in some ways, it is. But it also carries a cost. Because when your system is always trying to predict what is coming next, it rarely gets to fully settle in what is here.

Looking back, I can see that I became highly attuned to emotional shifts.

Tone.
Expression.
Silence.
Energy changes.

I would notice them quickly, often before anything had been said. And because I did not always understand what those shifts meant, I would try to interpret them.

Was something wrong?

Had I done something?

Was something about to happen?

That pattern followed me into later life.

It showed up in relationships, in conversations, in environments where nothing explicit had gone wrong, yet something felt off.

More often than not, I would look inward first. I would assume responsibility before questioning the situation more broadly.

That is one of the ways emotional formation continues into adulthood. Not just through memory, but through interpretation.

How we learned to make sense of early experiences becomes how we make sense of later ones.

If you learned that tension might mean you had done something wrong, you may continue to interpret it that way, even when the reality is more complex.

If you learned that connection required effort or adjustment, you may continue to work for it, even when it is not yours to manage.

If you learned that your feelings were too much, you may begin to filter them before they are even expressed.

None of this is conscious at first.

It becomes familiar.

Familiarity can feel like truth, even when it is not.

There were times in my life when I felt both deeply connected and deeply uncertain at the same time.

Connected enough to care.
Uncertain enough to question myself constantly.

That combination can be difficult to navigate because it creates a kind of internal tension.

You want to trust what you feel, but you have learned to doubt it.

You want to express what is real, but you are not sure how it will be received.

You want stability, but part of you is prepared for it to shift.

That is not a failure of character.

It is a continuation of the pattern.

Patterns do not disappear simply because we become older. They change shape.

They adapt to new environments.

They become more complex. But they are still there, influencing how we respond, how we interpret, how we relate.

There were also periods where I moved in the opposite direction.

Instead of heightened sensitivity, there was numbness.

Moments where I felt disconnected from what I was feeling. Not in a peaceful way, but in a muted way. As though something had been turned down or switched off. That, too, was confusing at the time. I could not always understand why I would move between intensity and absence, between feeling too much and feeling very little.

Now, I can see that both ends of that experience were part of the same system trying to regulate itself.

When things became too intense, there would be a shutdown. When things felt uncertain, there would be heightened awareness.

Neither was chosen consciously. Both were learned responses.

And because I did not understand that at the time, I often judged myself for both.

Too sensitive.
Too detached.
Too reactive.
Too withdrawn.

But those labels miss something important.

They describe the surface, but not the origin.

As I began to reflect more deeply, I also started to see how much of my identity had formed around these patterns.

Not just how I felt, but how I saw myself.

Am I difficult?
Am I too much?

Am I not enough?

Am I the problem here?

Those questions did not come from nowhere. They were shaped over time, through repeated experiences where my internal world did not seem to align with how it was received externally.

That creates a kind of fragmentation.

One part of you feels something clearly.
Another part questions whether it is valid.

One part wants to speak.
Another part hesitates.

One part recognises that something is not right.
Another part tries to maintain peace.

This is how inner conflict develops, not as a flaw, but as a consequence of navigating environments where clarity was not always available.

Yet, within all of that, there was also something else developing.

Awareness.

Not complete. Not stable. But present.

A growing sense that there was more to what I was experiencing than I had been taught to see. That my reactions, my patterns, my internal shifts were not random, even if I did not yet understand them fully.

That awareness did not arrive as certainty. It arrived as a notice.

As small moments of recognition.
As pauses where I began to observe rather than immediately react.
As questions that did not disappear as quickly as they once did.

And over time, that noticing began to create space.

Space between stimulus and response.
Space between feeling and interpretation.
Space between what I had learned and what I was beginning to see for myself.

That space is subtle, but it matters.

Because without it, everything feels immediate and fixed.

With it, something begins to shift.

Not all at once.
Not completely.

But enough to begin seeing patterns instead of only living inside them.

This chapter is not about resolving those patterns.

It is about recognising how they were formed.

How emotional life develops before we understand it.
How the nervous system learns from experience, not explanation.
How identity can grow around adaptation.

How sensitivity and shutdown can exist within the same person, not as a contradiction, but as a response.

Most importantly, how what feels like "who we are" is often, at least in part, what we have learned to be.

That recognition can be unsettling.

Because it raises a deeper question.

If so much of what I feel, how I react, and how I see myself has been shaped by experiences I did not choose...

Then what is actually mine?

That question does not need to be answered here.

But it does need to be asked. Because it leads directly into what comes next.

Chapter 7 - The Shadow Code

By the time patterns repeat often enough, they stop looking like patterns.

They begin to look like a personality.
Like preference.
Like fate.
Like the kind of relationships you "just end up in."
Like the way you "just are."

That is part of what makes this stage of the journey so difficult.

What was once an adaptation becomes so familiar that it starts to feel natural.

The hidden rules you learned early do not announce themselves as inheritance.

They move quietly beneath the surface, shaping what you expect, what you tolerate, what you explain away, what you fear, and what you keep returning to, even when some part of you already knows the return is costing too much.

That is what I mean by the shadow code:

the internal set of loyalties, responses, and emotional habits that continue running long after the original circumstances have changed.

Some of those rules were formed early and simply became normal to me. In my home, silence was often easier than continuing to press an issue.

I was told to be quiet. At times, the message was not to ask. At other times, it was not spoken directly, but the emotional atmosphere made the rule clear enough.

When tension rose, expression could intensify it.

So I learned, often without fully realising it, that quietness could be a way of surviving what could not yet be resolved.

Those kinds of rules do not disappear when childhood ends. They follow you.

They begin turning up in adult conversations, adult relationships, adult conflict, and adult fear. They begin shaping the distance between what you feel and what you allow yourself to say.

What is especially powerful about hidden rules is that they do not always feel imposed. Often, they feel practical. Necessary. Sensible.

They arrive as the most efficient way of getting through the moment. But practicality under pressure can become self-erasure over time.

When silence is repeatedly rewarded with less friction, the body starts to associate quietness with safety.

When overexplaining occasionally prevents abandonment, the mind starts to believe that more explanation might finally produce understanding.

When taking responsibility for everyone else's emotional state seems to reduce conflict, that becomes part of how love itself is interpreted.

None of this appears dramatic from the outside. But inwardly it builds a code. A private operating system.

There were also behaviours in my early environment that felt normal at the time because I had no alternative frame for them. Arguing. Shouting. Tension following mood changes.

A general sense that if someone became triggered, the atmosphere of the whole room could change. I knew, even then, that not everyone lived the same way, but familiarity can dull the shock of what would otherwise be recognised more clearly.

We become accustomed to emotional weather we would never have consciously chosen.

The difficulty is that what becomes normal in one stage of life often becomes the standard by which later experiences are interpreted.

A person can walk into adult relationships already primed to absorb instability as ordinary, to read emotional strain as inevitable, and to stay much longer than they should because some deeper part of them has mistaken familiarity for home.

This is where repetition becomes one of the clearest teachers.

Looking back on my relationships, I can see recurring patterns with painful clarity.

Overexplaining. Fear of abandonment. Becoming overly responsible. Shutting down. Staying too long. Trying to hold things together after it had become obvious that mutuality was no longer present.

Giving people chance after chance to treat me fairly while they continued dismissing what they were doing, dismissing my thoughts, my feelings, my beliefs, as though my reality needed constant negotiation while theirs was to be accepted without question.

That kind of repetition is exhausting, but more than that, it is revealing. It shows you what your system has been trained to keep hoping for. It shows you how long old bargains can survive inside adult love.

For me, one of the hardest things to admit was how often I stayed loyal to dynamics that had already shown me what they were.

I defended some of my own behaviours, yes, but I also defended the harmful behaviour of others for longer than I should have.

In certain relationships, I felt I had to take the lead, had to hold things together, had to keep working at the connection even while being told I was not doing enough.

There is a particular kind of loneliness in that position. You are carrying the relationship and being accused of failing it at the same time.

Over time, that creates a corrosive confusion.

You begin questioning your own integrity while doing most of the emotional labour.

You begin explaining more, enduring more, trying more, hoping that if you can only communicate clearly enough, prove yourself consistently enough, or remain patient long enough, the relationship will finally meet you where you are. But some dynamics are not waiting for clarity.

They are feeding on your willingness to keep making room for what they refuse to face in themselves.

That pattern is what made overexplaining such a significant part of this chapter for me. Overexplaining can look like openness, honesty, even maturity.

But often it comes from something more frightening than that. It comes from the fear that if you are not fully understood, you will be left.

It comes from the belief that if you can just present the truth cleanly enough, the other person will finally stop distorting it.

It comes from the hope that explanation can protect you from projection. But explanation has limits. Especially where people are more committed to defending themselves than to meeting reality together. I did not always know where that limit was, and because I did not, I crossed it often. I gave more words to situations than they deserved.

I tried to repair what was not mine alone to repair. I brought sincerity into rooms where sincerity was being used against me.

Fear of abandonment sat beneath much of that. Not always obviously.

Not always in panic. Sometimes it appeared simply as staying. As enduring what did not feel right because leaving felt heavier than carrying what was already hurting me.

At other times, it showed up as trying to remain emotionally available to people who were not capable of reciprocating that availability.

I became aware, with time, that some people loved being around me when I was strong, energised, supportive, and steady. But when I needed something in return, when the direction of care needed to move both ways, they disappeared.

They could draw from my stability, but not stand inside my difficulty.

That is a devastating pattern to wake up to, because it forces you to confront how often you have been valued not for who you are, but for what you could provide. Safety.

Energy. Patience. Presence. Reassurance. Once I saw that more clearly, I could no longer pretend not to know it.

There is also a deep shame that can build around perfectly human needs when those needs keep meeting the wrong environments.

The need to be understood.

The need to be met consistently.

The need to feel emotionally safe.

The need not to be dismissed.

When those needs go unanswered or get manipulated often enough, the person carrying them may begin to feel ashamed for having them at all.

It becomes easier to accuse yourself of being too much than to admit how little you have truly been given.

It becomes easier to frame your needs as a weakness than to face the fact that others have benefited from your willingness to shrink them.

That is how dysfunction becomes internalised. Not only through what happened to you, but through what you came to feel embarrassed for wanting.

By this stage in my life, I could also see more clearly that some of the people I had become entangled with were repeating patterns of their own.

Projection, dependency, emotional inconsistency, guilt, withdrawal, accusation, contradiction. I do not say that to flatten them into caricatures, but to acknowledge that unhealed people often draw one another into familiar pain.

One person overexplains. Another withholds.

One person tries harder. Another destabilises the ground beneath the conversation.

One person carries responsibility. Another escapes it. These pairings can become strangely magnetic because they fit codes both people already know, even while hurting them. That is one of the darker aspects of repetition: pain can feel like recognition, and recognition can be mistaken for love.

At the same time, I do not want this chapter to suggest that I was merely a passive recipient of harmful dynamics.

Part of the shadow code is the part you participate in. The part that stays. The part that excuses.

The part that keeps hoping the pattern will break without you having to step outside it. I had to face that too. I had to admit how often I kept extending myself into situations that had already shown me their limits.

I had to admit how often I was still trying to win fairness from places committed to distortion.

That is not comfortable work, because it asks you to let go not only of what was done to you, but of the image you had of yourself as someone who was simply enduring and not, in some way, collaborating with what no longer served you.

Ownership is difficult because it removes fantasy. But it also returns power.

The more I saw these patterns, the more I understood why shutdown had remained so close to me. Shutdown is not only a nervous-system event.

It can also become a relational position. A retreat. A final boundary when explanation has failed, when fairness has failed, when openness has failed, when staying available has only made you more vulnerable to misuse.

There were many times in my life when I went quiet, not because I had nothing to say, but because continuing to say it no longer honoured me.

Silence, in those moments, was not always avoidance. Sometimes it was the only remaining dignity available. Sometimes it was the body refusing one more round of distortion. Sometimes it was the soul withdrawing from a field that could no longer meet it honestly.

Yet, even as I write that, I can see the complexity. Because silence has served different roles in my life. It has been protected.

It has been repression.

It has been wisdom.

It has been fear.

It has been a refuge.

It has also been a prison.

That is the difficulty with inherited patterns: they are not always simple enough to reject wholesale.

The same strategy that once kept you safe may later keep you small. The same sensitivity that once overwhelmed you may later become discernment.

The same caution that once reflected fear may later become clarity.

The work, then, is not merely to throw away all the old patterns, but to understand which part of each pattern belongs to survival and which part can be transformed into something more conscious.

This chapter sits at the point in the journey where repetition becomes impossible to romanticise.

The code is no longer hidden enough to pretend it is simply "bad luck" or "the wrong people" or "another misunderstanding." By now, the deeper question is unavoidable.

What have I been repeating?

What have I been protecting?

What have I been expecting from myself that I would never demand from someone I truly loved?

What have I called loyalty that was really fear? What have I called patience that was really self-abandonment?

Those questions do not arrive gently, but they are necessary. Because without them, the shadow remains abstract. With them, it becomes visible.

I know now that I no longer want to live by that old code. I no longer want to chase understanding from people committed to misunderstanding me.

I no longer want to mistake being needed for being loved.

I no longer want to over-explain my reality to make it palatable to those who benefit from denying it.

I no longer want to carry responsibilities that belong equally, or entirely, to others.

That is part of why I have chosen peace more deliberately now.

Not because I no longer care. Not because I have become cold. But because I have finally learned that preserving my energy, my dignity, and my nervous system is not selfish. It is necessary.

If Part I revealed the fracture, and the first chapters of Part II revealed how that fracture lived in the body and in emotional formation, then this chapter reveals how it kept trying to recreate itself through relationships.

The shadow code is not only about old pain. It is about the way old pain organises the future until it is recognised clearly enough to be interrupted.

That is why this chapter matters. Because once the pattern is visible, the next stage of the journey can begin. Not the easy stage. Not the resolved stage. But the stage where you stop asking only why this keeps happening and start asking something far more demanding: What, in me, still mistakes familiarity for truth?

Chapter 8 - The Myth of the Rational Mind

One of the more unsettling truths I had to face was that knowing something is wrong does not always mean you can leave it immediately.

For a long time, I wanted to believe that reason would save me.

If I could think clearly enough, analyse carefully enough, explain honestly enough, then I could either resolve what was happening or at least protect myself from becoming lost inside it. I trusted my ability to reflect. I trusted my ability to observe. I trusted that if something was inconsistent, irrational, unfair, or emotionally manipulative, then seeing it clearly would be enough to free me from it.

But life does not always work that way.

There were moments when I knew something was not right and stayed anyway. Not because I was blind. Not because I lacked intelligence.

Not because I enjoyed pain. I stayed because knowing and acting are not always born in the same part of us.

One part can recognise the truth while another part still hopes, still explains, still waits, still tries to preserve the connection, still wants one more conversation, one more clarification, one more chance for things to become what they claimed to be.

That gap between recognition and release became one of the most important things I had to understand in myself. It showed me that the rational mind is not sovereign in the way we often pretend it is. It does not simply issue a verdict, and the rest of the self falls into line.

When I think about one particular relationship, I can see this very clearly. From early on, I felt something was off. I could not explain it properly at first.

There was no clean sentence I could point to, no singular event dramatic enough to justify the depth of the unease. But something in me knew. Something in me registered inconsistency, misattunement, the quiet wrongness of a field that never fully settled. And yet I stayed.

I moved through nearly three years of what would become an exhausting and often deeply destabilising experience, not because I lacked perception, but because perception alone did not immediately undo the old forces moving underneath it. Hope stayed. Explanation stayed.

The desire to work through things stayed. The old conditioning that said perhaps if you just remain patient enough, speak clearly enough, love steadily enough, things might finally become mutual — that stayed too.

That is one of the great myths about rationality: that once you know, you are free.

Often, you are not free yet. Often, you are only at the beginning of another kind of struggle.

Because what keeps a person in confusion is not always a lack of information. Sometimes it is an emotional investment. Sometimes it is fear. Sometimes it is history.

Sometimes it is the pull of familiar pain. Sometimes it is the hope that this time the old pattern will end differently. Sometimes, it is the nervous system still orienting around the connection even when the connection itself has become harmful.

The mind may know, but the body may still be trying to preserve attachment. The intellect may see contradiction, but another part of the self may still be trying to avoid the grief of letting go.

I had to learn that painful lesson in real time.

There were arguments where facts did not matter. Situations where what was true in the plainest sense could be denied, twisted, or reframed depending on what the other person needed to protect themselves.

At times, it was surreal to witness. At times embarrassing.

At times exhausting beyond words. I would find myself looking at something that felt completely clear, something anybody could see, and still the conversation would move as though reality itself was negotiable. That was not just frustrating. It was destabilising. It forced me to confront how little reason alone can do when emotion, fear, projection, and ego are driving the exchange. Clear thinking does not disappear in those moments, but it becomes trapped inside a field where clarity is not what the other person is defending. They are defending identity, self-image, control, avoidance, and the right not to have to face themselves. Facts, then, become secondary.

That shook something in me because, for much of my life, I had believed that truth spoken sincerely ought to matter. Not that everyone would like it, but it would at least have a chance of landing.

What I had to face was that truth does not land equally in all nervous systems. Some people hear a challenge where there is only a difference. Some hear accusation where there is only honesty. Some hear a threat where there is only reflection. When a person is emotionally defended, language itself changes function.

It no longer becomes a bridge between realities. It becomes material for defence. Material for deflection. Material for counter-attack. That is difficult to live with if you are still hoping understanding can be reached simply by refining the sentence.

At some point, you have to accept that not every conversation is failing because you have not explained yourself well enough. Some conversations fail because the other person is not truly available to reality while they are protecting something more fundamental in themselves.

There is also something humbling in this chapter, because I do not want to make it sound as though I was some detached witness to irrationality in others while remaining entirely above it myself. I was not. My own emotions had shaped my reasoning, too.

There were times when fear distorted what I was willing to see clearly. Times when wanting the relationship to work kept me seated longer than my deeper knowing had wanted.

Times when my own history of misunderstanding, abandonment, fear, and people-pleasing softened what should have been a firmer boundary. I can say now that I was aware something was wrong, but I must also say that awareness and embodiment were not yet aligned.

I knew, but I had not yet fully trusted what I knew. And until trust enters, knowledge can remain strangely powerless.

This is why the phrase *the rational mind* needs questioning.

We often speak as though the mind is either rational or irrational, as though these are clean categories. But what I experienced was far more layered than that.

A person can reason brilliantly in some areas of life and still become emotionally entangled in others. A person can analyse social systems, political structures, patterns of behaviour, or philosophical questions with real depth while remaining caught inside a relationship that is quietly undoing them.

That is not hypocrisy in the shallow sense. It is the complexity of being human. The mind is not floating above the body, issuing neutral judgements untouched by history. It is in relationship with memory, attachment, pain, desire, fear, physiology, hope, fantasy, and survival.

Reason is never as pure as people like to imagine. It is constantly being shaped by the state.

That became more obvious to me as my own awakening deepened. I started seeing more clearly how many beliefs or behaviours I had once accepted as normal no longer made sense once I stepped back from them.

I began to see how much of what is presented as truth in the world is sustained not because it is coherent, but because people are emotionally invested in keeping it intact.

Systems, identities, relationships, cultural assumptions, social performances, these things do not survive by logic alone.

They survive because they are bonded to emotional needs. The need to belong. The need to feel safe. The need to remain superior.

The need not to feel foolish. The need not to confront complicity. The need not to grieve what reality would cost if it were faced honestly.

That is true at the personal level and the collective level. Reason, then, is rarely operating in a vacuum. It often serves a deeper emotional economy, whether the person recognises that or not.

I had to see that in myself too.

There were times I had told myself stories about why I was still where I was. Stories that sounded thoughtful, compassionate, and mature.

Perhaps I am being too harsh. Perhaps they are just hurting. Perhaps if I communicate differently. Perhaps if I hold steady. Perhaps if I detach more. Perhaps if I become calmer. Some of those thoughts were not false in themselves. The problem was that they were often being used not only to understand the situation, but to prolong my stay inside it.

Rationality, in that sense, can become another form of delay. Another strategy for not yet acting on what the body and intuition have already begun to know. Thought can become a waiting room where grief is postponed.

There is a kind of exhaustion that comes from this.

Not the exhaustion of thinking too much in a general sense, but the exhaustion of trying to think your way through what can only finally be resolved by deeper honesty. I know that feeling well.

The looping. The replaying. The mental effort to find the missing piece that will finally make the whole thing coherent. But some situations are not waiting to be solved. They are waiting to be seen for what they are. There comes a point when the mind must stop trying to rescue the illusion of coherence and admit that what is happening is incoherent because the dynamic itself is incoherent. In those moments, more thought does not always bring relief. Sometimes it only deepens the trap.

That recognition did not make me anti-rational. If anything, it made me value reason more properly. It showed me that reason has a vital role, but only when it is honest about its limits.

The rational mind is invaluable when it helps name contradictions, trace patterns, recognise inconsistency, and resist emotional capture. But it becomes dangerous when it imagines itself independent of embodiment, history, or state.

It becomes a mask when it denies the role of pain in shaping what it is willing to conclude. It becomes another defence when it treats emotional reality as noise rather than part of the field that must be understood.

I suppose that is the deeper movement of this chapter. Not the rejection of reason, but its reorientation. It's humbling. It's a return to proportion.

I no longer believe that clarity is just a matter of intellectual strength. I believe clarity requires alignment. The mind must think, yes, but the body must also be heard. Intuition must not be overridden too quickly. Emotional investment must be recognised.

Fear must be named. History must be acknowledged. Otherwise, what we call rationality may be little more than thought serving an old wound while pretending to be objective.

That is a difficult truth, because it means the work goes deeper than argument. Deeper than information. Deeper than being right. It means a person can know many things and still not be free. It means the journey through darkness is not resolved by intelligence alone.

It requires something more demanding than that. It requires the courage to see where thought has been protecting pain rather than exposing it.

It requires the humility to admit that the mind is not always captain, and that what we have called logic has sometimes been another form of survival.

By the time I reached this point, I could feel that something was changing in me. The old certainty that if I could just understand enough,

I would finally resolve everything that had begun to fall away. In its place was something less grand but more honest. A quieter recognition that truth is not only something to think about. It is something to live with.

Something to act on. Something to trust even when the rational mind is still trying to negotiate with what the deeper self already knows.

That shift matters because it prepares the ground for what comes next.

If this chapter is about the collapse of the fantasy that reason alone can save us, then the next chapter enters the space that often opens once that fantasy has fallen. The silence after the arguing.

The loneliness after the pattern becomes undeniable. The collapse of the old explanations. The in-between place where the self is no longer willing to pretend, but has not yet fully rebuilt itself around a deeper truth.

That is where the darkness becomes quieter, but no less profound.

That is where the journey enters the void.

Chapter 9 - Silence, Isolation, and the Void

There comes a point in some journeys where the noise stops, not because everything has been resolved, but because there is nothing left in you that can keep performing the old arguments.

The explanations begin to thin out.
The justifications lose their force.
The compulsive need to keep making sense of what has already wounded you begins to collapse under its own weight.

What remains then is not peace, at least not at first.

What remains is silence.

Not the gentle kind.
Not the chosen kind.
Not the silence of rest.

But the silence that follows exhaustion. The silence that arrives when too much has been lost, too much has been seen, too much has been carried, and something in you can no longer keep pretending that movement alone is progress.

That was the terrain I entered more than once in my life: a quieter darkness, but in some ways a more confronting one than anything that had come before it. Because when the noise falls away, there is nowhere left to hide from what is still there.

I had known silence before, of course. Silence had been part of my life since childhood. It served many functions. It had been protection when speech felt unsafe. It had been withdrawn when tension was too much to metabolise. It had been a shield against misunderstanding, against conflict, against being drawn further into emotional fields that already felt too charged.

Earlier in life, silence often meant bracing, retreating, and reducing my exposure to what I did not know how to handle. It was linked to safety, or at least to the nearest thing I had to safety at the time.

But the silence I entered here was different.

It was not only defensive. It was existential.

It came in the aftermath of patterns becoming impossible to deny.

It came when relationships had stripped away too much illusion.

It came when the body had already been speaking loudly for a long time, when the mind had exhausted its attempts to reason with what should never have required that much reasoning, and when some deeper part of me could no longer participate in my own confusion with the same enthusiasm.

That kind of silence does not feel immediately holy. It feels empty. It feels stripped back. It feels like a life once filled with motion has suddenly become too spacious in all the wrong ways.

Loneliness lives differently in a space like that.

There is the ordinary loneliness of missing people, missing company, missing warmth, missing the easy comfort of being around others. But there is also a deeper loneliness that comes when the self you had organised your life around begins to fall away.

A loneliness not only of company, but of identity. Of no longer being who you were in the old dynamics, and not yet knowing who you are without them. That is a much harder state to describe, because it is not solved simply by being around more people.

In some ways, being around the wrong people intensifies it. You can be surrounded and still feel profoundly alone when the self that once adapted to belonging is beginning to refuse the old terms of belonging.

I know now that much of this loneliness belonged to the in-between state.

That is perhaps the clearest phrase for it: the in-between.

The place where the old self no longer fits, but the new self has not yet stabilised. The place where the old strategies have lost credibility, but nothing solid has fully replaced them.

The place where you can no longer wholeheartedly return to who you were, but you do not yet know how to live from what you are becoming.

That state is deeply unsettling because human beings like continuity. We like to know who we are. We like familiar patterns, even painful ones, if they let us retain a coherent identity. The void threatens that coherence. It asks for something far more difficult than explanation. It asks for surrender.

I did not always welcome that.

There were times when I still wanted to reach backwards, to revive what was already over, to reanimate the old explanations, to find a final sentence that would let me leave the darkness neatly rather than pass through it. But some seasons of life do not end through one perfect insight.

They end through depletion. Through realising there is simply no life left in what you have been trying to preserve. Through recognising that what you have called hope has begun to function as a delay.

Through coming to terms with the fact that certain rooms, certain dynamics, certain versions of yourself cannot be carried any further without costing you too much of what remains.

and when that recognition settles, silence deepens.

What makes the void so difficult is that it does not reward performance. It does not respond to overexplaining. It is not impressed by spiritual language, intellectual analysis, or the image you still have of yourself as someone who can think their way through everything.

The void strips away all of that. It leaves you with your own presence, or the lack of it. It leaves you with what remains when the distractions have thinned out, and the old identities no longer sustain themselves so easily. In that sense, the void is brutal, but it is honest. It does not flatter. It does not entertain. It reveals.

I spent time in that kind of space more than once. There were periods where I withdrew from noise, from people, from the pressure to keep performing social coherence. Some of that withdrawal was necessary. Some of it was painful.

Some of it carried relief I did not yet know how to trust. I had been around enough contradiction, enough emotional instability, enough energetic confusion to know that silence, however hard, could still be less damaging than remaining embedded in fields that kept distorting me.

That, too, is part of the paradox of isolation: sometimes it hurts, but sometimes it also protects what little clarity you still have left.

Nature became important to me in those times. So did the quiet movement. Walking. Being outside.

Time away from the emotional density of certain environments.

Those spaces did not always give me answers, but they gave me room. They allowed the body to downshift.

They gave the mind less to fight with. They gave me intervals in which I could hear myself again, however faintly. Looking back, I do not think I understood fully then just how necessary that was.

I only knew that some places made me feel more whole than others, and that stepping away from noise was not always avoidable. Sometimes it was the first act of honesty available to me.

There is a kind of grief that belongs specifically to this stage of a journey.

Not only grief for people or events, but grief for the selves that no longer survive contact with deeper truth. Grief for the part of you that kept trying.

Grief for the part that stayed too long.

Grief for the image you had of how things were meant to unfold.

Grief for the years spent making room for dynamics that were never going to become what they promised.

Grief for the time, the energy, the innocence, the trust, the emotional labour.

The void brings all of that closer because it no longer lets you remain as distracted from your own losses. Yet there is something necessary in that grief. It clears the ground. It tells the truth about what mattered.

It releases the need to stay artificially strong in the face of things that have, in fact, cost you.

What changed for me, slowly, was that silence stopped being only a defence.

It began to become a place of listening.

That did not happen instantly. At first, silence still carried residue: old arguments, replayed conversations, emotional aftershocks, unfinished thoughts, bodily tension.

But with time, and with enough distance from the things that had been distorting my inner world, the quality of that silence began to change. I noticed that not everything required a response.

Not every provocation required engagement. Not every misunderstanding required another attempt at repair. Not every loss required immediate replacement. There was a subtle but profound shift in that. Silence was no longer only where I disappeared. It was where I returned.

That is one of the deepest paradoxes of this chapter.

The silence that once represented shutdown can, in another season of life, become the very place where deeper truth starts to gather.

What once meant withdrawal can become discernment.
What once meant emptiness can become spaciousness.
What once meant collapse can become a clearing.

But none of that is available if the void is rushed. If a person hurries too quickly to rebuild, too quickly to become "better," too quickly to put a spiritual narrative over a human unravelling, they miss the depth of what this stage is actually doing. The void is not punishment. It is not a failure. It is not proof that life has gone wrong. It is often the interval in which the old architecture finally comes down enough for something truer to be built. I think that is why this chapter has to sit where it does.

Part II has been about the darkness, not as drama, but as confrontation. The body speaks louder. Emotional formation coming into view. Repetition in relationships is becoming undeniable. The rational mind is losing its fantasy of sovereignty. This chapter brings all of that to its deepest still point.

It does not resolve the darkness, but it changes its texture. The darkness becomes quieter here, more stripped back, less argumentative, more exposing. It is no longer only about what happened. It is about what remains when what happened can no longer be hidden behind movement.

If Part I asked where the fracture began, and Part II asked what that fracture has been doing inside me all this time, then this chapter leaves me with another question, quieter and more demanding than the ones before it:

Who am I when I am no longer busy surviving what has already ended?

That question does not arrive with an immediate answer. It arrives like the edge of dawn before the light can yet be trusted. It arrives as something sensed rather than fully known. And perhaps that is how the shift begins. Not in triumph. Not in Revelation. But in the first honest stillness after the old noise has collapsed.

That is where Part II closes. Not with certainty. Not with completion. But with a threshold. The darkness has not vanished. But something in it has changed. The confrontation has done its work.

What was hidden has come forward. What was carried unconsciously has become harder to deny. What was once only pain has begun, however faintly, to turn into awareness. And awareness, at first, is rarely dramatic. It arrives quietly.

Part III - The Shift

There is a point in some journeys where the darkness stops being only something you are trapped inside and starts becoming something you can observe.

That point does not usually arrive with spectacle. It does not announce itself as a dramatic rebirth. It does not suddenly make the past simple, the body settled, or the future clear.

More often, it begins in quieter ways than that. In pauses. I noticed. In the first fragile experiences of not being completely fused with every reaction, every fear, every inherited pattern. This is the beginning of the shift.

If Part II was the confrontation, then Part III is the gradual reorientation that follows it.

Not escape from darkness, but a changed relationship to it. Not perfection, but perception. Not a finished self, but the early formation of a more honest one.

This section moves more quietly for a reason. It is not trying to overpower what came before. It is trying to show how something begins to soften, clarify, and reassemble once the old certainties have fallen away.

This is where awareness begins to gather enough stability to become a new ground. It is still subtle. Still human. Still uneven. But it is real.

What changes here is not that the past disappears. It is that it can no longer dominate experience in quite the same unconscious way. There begins to be space.

Space to notice a pattern instead of only becoming it. Space to recognise what belongs to the body, what belongs to old fear, what belongs to habit, and what belongs to the present.

Space to see that some of what once felt like identity was adaptation. Space to trust certain signals without being swallowed by them.

This is where the reader begins to feel space, breath, and movement again.

Not instant salvation, but growing clarity. Not a perfected life, but the first real signs of spiritual coherence beginning to form from within lived experience. The chapters that follow trace that change carefully.

Chapter 10 - Awareness Arrives Quietly

This chapter marks the first real turn in the book. It explores awakening not as a single revelation, but as a gradual process of small realisations and a subtle return to self.

It moves through the earliest moments of noticing your own patterns, recognising that reactions are happening before conscious thought, and becoming a witness to your own internal state.

This is where grounded self-awareness first begins to take shape.

Chapter 11 - Seeing the Patterns

This chapter deepens awareness into recognition. It explores recurring relational dynamics, language and perception, thought loops, and the more hidden forms of self-betrayal that keep old wounds alive.

It traces how certain dynamics repeated across relationships and environments, how tone, implication, and dismissal shaped perception, and how the same wound can keep returning in different forms.

This chapter lightly and naturally connects your personal journey with your broader insights.

Chapter 12 - The Body Knows Before the Mind

This chapter returns to the body from a new place. No longer only the site of pain, it becomes the ground of discernment. It explores intuition, nervous-system awareness, the signals of safety and threat, and the process of reconnecting with embodied truth.

It moves through learning to trust physical cues, breath, heartbeat, posture, energetic shifts, and the role of nature and stillness in regulation. This is where awakening becomes embodied, not just intellectual.

Chapter 13 - Letting Go of Who I Was

This chapter becomes the inner turning point of the section. It explores identity release, the ending of performance, the grief of old selves, and the movement towards acceptance without defeat.

It turns towards letting go of validation-seeking, releasing unhealthy relational loops, refusing false peace, and no longer building life around being understood by everyone. This is where the self begins to stop begging the world for permission to exist.

Part III matters because it is where the journey begins to move from collapse towards coherence, from survival towards discernment, and from constant reaction towards the first more grounded forms of inner participation.

If Part II asked, What has this been doing inside me all this time?
Then Part III begins to ask something new:

What becomes possible now that I can finally see it?

Like so much that matters in life, that answer begins quietly.

Chapter 10 - Awareness Arrives Quietly

I used to think that change would announce itself.

That if something in me was truly shifting, I would know it dramatically. I imagined awakening, in the abstract, as a kind of event. A breakthrough. A revelation. A moment so clear and undeniable that everything before it would be divided neatly from everything after it. The darkness would be one chapter. The light another. Confusion would end. Clarity would begin. The old self would fall away, and a new one would rise with certainty enough to recognise itself immediately.

But that was not how it happened for me.

What changed first did not feel grand. It felt subtle. Almost easy to overlook. It arrived not as a finished answer, but as a slight difference in how I was meeting my own experience. A little more space. A little more notice. A little less total fusion with what I was feeling at the moment. That may sound small, but it was not small. It was the beginning of an entirely different relationship with myself.

Before that, much of my life had been lived from within reaction. Not because I wanted it that way, but because so much of what I carried had been operating beneath the surface. I would feel, and then become the feeling. I would react, and only later reflect. I would get pulled into the atmosphere of a room, the emotional weight of an interaction, the pressure of a pattern, and by the time I was aware of what had happened, I was already inside it. That had been true for years. So when a different quality of awareness began to emerge, it did not feel like fireworks. It felt like the first moment of standing half a step back from what had always seemed immediate.

I began to notice things I had previously only lived through.

That was the shift.

I noticed how quickly my body changed in certain situations. I noticed how my mind rushed to interpret other people's moods. I noticed the familiar internal tightening when a conversation turned uncertain. I noticed how often my energy responded before my thoughts formed fully. I noticed the old urge to explain, the old urge to maintain peace, the old urge to doubt myself before doubting the situation. None of those things disappeared overnight. But I was no longer only inside them. I was beginning, however inconsistently, to witness them.

That distinction changed everything.

To witness is not to detach coldly. It is not to become numb or removed. It is something more alive than that. It is the beginning of being present enough to see what is happening without immediately being consumed by it. That kind of presence did not come naturally to me at first. It had to grow. It had to be practised. It had to be protected. But once it began, I could feel the difference. I was no longer entirely at the mercy of every internal shift. I was starting to recognise movement inside myself as movement, rather than as absolute truth.

That was both relieving and unsettling.

Relieving, because it gave me space. Unsettling, because it forced me to see how much of my life I had spent without that space.

There is a strange grief that comes with growing awareness. People often speak of awakening as though it is only liberating, but that is not the full truth. Sometimes awareness brings relief, yes, but it also brings the pain of seeing clearly what you had once normalised.

It brings the ache of recognising how often you left yourself, how often you stayed too long, how often you argued with your own intuition, how often you confused survival with wisdom. In that sense, awareness does not only soothe. It exposes. It shows you what has been there all along.

Still, I would not trade it.

Because even when awareness hurt, it gave me something I had been missing for years: a point of contact with myself that did not rely on external agreement.

That mattered deeply.

For so much of my life, being understood by others had carried enormous weight. Not because I needed to be admired, but because I had spent so long feeling unseen, misread, or reorganised by other people's interpretations.

The deeper the patterns became, the more exhausting that was. So when awareness began to gather, one of its quiet gifts was this: I started needing less external confirmation to know what I was feeling. I did not become arrogant. I did not become closed. But I became less willing to abandon my own perception simply because someone else was uncomfortable with it.

That was not a loud change. It did not make me more forceful. If anything, it made me quieter in a different way.

Less reactive.
Less eager to prove.
Less desperate to be met by those who had no real intention of meeting me.

Awareness changed the quality of my attention. I began to notice where my energy went. I began to notice which environments left me more settled and which left me fragmented.

I began to notice the difference between genuine peace and suppression masquerading as peace. I began to notice that some people made me feel expanded, clearer, more present in myself, while others left me compressed, uncertain, and subtly braced.

These things had always been happening. The shift was that I was now seeing them with more consistency.

It is difficult to explain just how powerful that kind of noticing can be when it first starts to stabilise.

Noticing is not glamorous. It does not look like mastery. It does not always produce immediate action. But it creates a new foundation. Because once you see a pattern clearly enough, you cannot fully return to the innocence of not seeing it. Once you notice how your body contracts around certain people, or how your thoughts begin racing in certain fields, or how your energy falls after particular interactions, that information stays with you.

You may not act on it perfectly. You may still hesitate. You may still have much to learn. But something has changed. The old unconsciousness has been interrupted.

I think that is why awareness arrived quietly for me. It needed to.

Had it come as some overwhelming revelation, I might have tried to turn it into an identity too quickly. I might have tried to become "the awakened version" of myself before I had actually learned how to live from that place.

But the quieter arrival of awareness protected me from that. It kept the process honest. It forced me to grow with it rather than perform it. It allowed the shift to remain lived rather than claimed.

And that mattered, because there is a subtle trap in speaking about awakening. The ego can try to wear it. It can turn a fragile, sacred process of becoming more honest into a new image of superiority.

I did not want that. Or rather, life had already shown me enough about illusion to know that I could not afford another one. What was happening to me was not a reason to feel above anyone. It was a reason to become more careful. More present. More willing to see. More willing to acknowledge how much of what I had once called "myself" had really been reaction, inheritance, adaptation, defence.

That is another reason this chapter matters. Because awareness does not only reveal the world differently. It reveals the self differently, too.

I started to see that some parts of me were not as fixed as I had once thought. Some reactions that had felt essential were patterned. Some fears that had felt definitive were old. Some identities I had worn were built around protection rather than truth. This did not leave me feeling empty. It left me feeling invited. Invited into a more careful examination of what was truly mine and what had simply become familiar through repetition.

That question became more and more central:

What in me is deeply true, and what in me was learned under pressure?

Awareness did not answer that all at once. But it made the question unavoidable.

There were moments where this shift felt almost painfully simple. I would notice I was beginning to tighten in a conversation. I would notice my body reacting before I had consciously decided what I thought. I would notice the old emotional momentum gathering. And instead of immediately becoming it, I would pause. Just for a second sometimes. But the pause was enough to change the shape of the moment. Enough to remind me that reaction was not my only option. Enough to create a little distance between stimulus and identity.

That distance is sacred in ways I do not use that word lightly to describe. Because at that distance, a person begins to recover choice.

Not total choice, not instant mastery, but the beginning of it.

The old patterns still had force. The body still had memory. The darkness had not vanished. But awareness had entered the field, and once it does, everything begins to reorganise around it.

I also began to experience moments of peace that were different from the peace I had once confused with shutting down. Earlier in life, there were times I thought I was calm when really I was simply withdrawn, numb, or tired of fighting. But now there were moments of a different quality altogether. Moments where I was not suppressing anything, not trying to control anything, not performing any version of steadiness. I was just present.

The body felt less divided. The mind is less noisy. The need to explain is less urgent. Those moments did not last forever, but they told me something important. They told me that peace was not the same as disappearance. It was possible to remain in myself without being at war with what I felt.

That was new.

And because it was new, it needed tenderness.

This stage of the journey is easily underestimated. From the outside, it may not look like much has changed. A person may still be living in the same world, doing the same ordinary things, carrying some of the same wounds, facing some of the same challenges. But internally, something has begun to reassemble. Attention is changing. Perception is changing. The relationship to reaction is changing. The self is beginning to gather around a quieter centre.

That is what this chapter honours.

Not a dramatic transformation.
Not final enlightenment.
Not a perfected version of self.

But the first honest signs that the system is no longer entirely unconscious of itself.

If Part II brought me into confrontation with what had been buried, this chapter marks the beginning of a different movement.

Not away from depth, but into a more stable relationship with it. The darkness has not ended, but it is no longer only something happening to me. I am beginning to see it. Beginning to track it. Beginning to recognise what rises, what tightens, what repeats, what softens, what is old, what is present, what is fear, what is truth.

That is enough for a beginning.

Perhaps that is the real nature of awakening, at least in its first form. Not a lightning strike. Not a total redefinition. But a quieter return.

A soft but unmistakable shift from living entirely inside your patterns to slowly becoming conscious of them.

A movement from possession to presence. From automaticity to attention. From being swept away by every old current to beginning, at last, to feel the water while remaining yourself.

That is how it arrived for me.

Quietly.
Gradually.
Without spectacle.

Because it came that way, I was able to trust it.

Chapter 11 - Seeing the Patterns

There is a difference between suffering and recognising the shape of suffering.

For a long time, I was living inside patterns I could feel but could not fully name. I knew certain situations affected me more deeply than others. I knew certain people left me unsettled in ways that stayed long after the interaction had ended.

I knew I found myself in familiar emotional positions again and again, overexplaining, doubting myself, trying to preserve peace, staying too long, feeling the old tension rise in new rooms. But knowing that something keeps happening is not the same as seeing the pattern beneath it.

That came later.

And when it did come, it changed the way I understood almost everything.

Because once a pattern is seen clearly enough, what once looked like isolated incidents begins to reveal itself as repetition.

Not bad luck.
Not random chemistry.
Not simply "the wrong person" again.
Not another unrelated misunderstanding.

But recurrence.

The same wound finds new language.

The same fear wears different faces.

The same internal position is being activated in different environments until it starts to become impossible to deny that the common thread is not only out there. It is also in here, in how I have learned to read, respond, tolerate, interpret, soften, defend, explain, and remain.

That recognition is not comfortable. But it is liberating.

Before I could see patterns clearly, I was often too close to the moment. Something would happen, and I would enter it immediately. I would focus on the event itself, the conversation, the argument, the behaviour, the tension. My attention would go to the immediate content of the experience.

What was said. What was done. What should I do now? Whether I had handled it well. Whether I needed to explain more. Whether I had misunderstood. Whether I was being too sensitive. The mind, once activated, would move around the moment itself with great intensity.

But pattern recognition requires a different kind of attention.

It asks you to step back enough to notice not only what is happening, but what kind of thing keeps happening. It asks you to stop treating each moment as entirely self-contained and begin asking harder questions. Why does this feel so familiar? Why do I keep arriving in this emotional position? Why do different people produce a strangely similar collapse in me?

Why does my body seem to know the script before the conversation has even fully begun?

That is when the shift deepens.

Because the first stage of awareness shows you that you are reacting. The next stage begins to show you what you are reacting *to*.

I started to notice recurring relational dynamics with increasing clarity. There were people who, on the surface, were quite different from one another, and yet something about the internal structure of the relationship felt the same. The same imbalance.

The same emotional labour. The same pressure to explain. The same subtle destabilisation of my reality.

The same experience of being close enough to care deeply, yet far enough from genuine safety that some part of me never fully settled.

What changed was not that these dynamics suddenly appeared. It was that I could no longer pretend they were unrelated.

Patterns began showing themselves across relationships, family environments, workspaces, social interactions, and even inner dialogue.

That last one mattered more than I first realised.

Because some of the deepest patterns were not only relational in the obvious sense. They had become internal. I was carrying ways of speaking to myself that had been shaped by years of misunderstanding, adaptation, and emotional strain. I noticed how quickly I would move to self-questioning.

How readily I would search for the part of the problem that must be mine. How often I would minimise what I felt until the feeling became too large to minimise any longer. How easily I would offer generosity to others while becoming suspicious of my own needs.

These patterns did not always sound dramatic in language, but they had dramatic consequences in life. They affected where I stayed, what I accepted, how long I waited, and how much of myself I gave away while still calling it patience.

That is part of why seeing the patterns felt both painful and necessary.

Painful, because it meant I had to grieve how much of my life had been shaped by repetition I did not fully understand. Necessary, because without seeing it, I would have remained loyal to forces that were quietly undoing me.

I also began to notice more clearly the role of language.

Not language in the abstract, but language as it actually lives between people. Tone. Timing. Implication. The things suggested but not stated. The subtle ways reality can be shaped not only by what is said, but by what is withheld, softened, redirected, dismissed, or loaded emotionally. There were interactions in my life where the words alone might not have seemed enough to explain the level of disturbance I felt. But once I began paying attention to the wider field of communication, the pattern became clearer. It was not only the content. It was the delivery. The atmosphere around the sentence.

The body language contradicts the reassurance. The silence that followed something important. The implication is hidden inside a casual remark. The tone that carried dismissal before the mind had fully caught up with what the body had already registered.

This was important for me because so much of my life had involved the experience of feeling something was off without being able to prove it cleanly enough for others to recognise it.

Pattern recognition changed that.

Not because it gave me some magical certainty, but because it taught me to take the accumulation of subtle things seriously. One moment of dismissal may not mean much in isolation. One contradiction might be explainable.

One uncomfortable interaction can happen anywhere. But patterns are made of accumulation. Repeated tones. Repeated evasions. Repeated emotional shifts. Repeated experiences of leaving an interaction more confused than when you entered it. Repeated pressure to mistrust your own perception while making room for everyone else's. That is where meaning begins to gather.

Once I started seeing that more clearly, something else became undeniable: the same wound had been wearing different faces for years.

That was one of the hardest truths to face.

I had thought, at various times, that I was dealing with entirely different people, entirely different situations, entirely different forms of pain. And in one sense, that was true. Each person was themselves. Each relationship had its own detail. Each moment had its own reality. But beneath those surface differences, the emotional structure often carried a strange familiarity.

The old wound of not being met. The old wound of trying to explain truth into a space more invested in defending itself. The old wound of being valued when useful but not held when vulnerable.

The old wound of feeling something real and then having to fight for its legitimacy. The old wound of being drawn into fields where my intuition stirred early, but some other part of me stayed seated longer than it should have.

Seeing that was sobering.

Because once you realise the same wound has kept reappearing, you have to ask a more demanding question than, *Why do people keep doing this?*

You have to ask, *What in me still recognises this as familiar enough to remain?*

That question is not self-blame. At least, not if approached honestly. It is not about turning all responsibility inward and excusing the harm of others. It is about understanding how old pain can create channels of familiarity, and how those channels influence what we accept, what we endure, what we hope for, and what we repeatedly mistake for connection.

I could see this not only in relationships, but in my own thought loops.

Certain mental loops had accompanied me for years. Trying to make sense of why someone had behaved the way they had. Replaying conversations. Revisiting moments of tension to search for the hidden explanation that would finally settle the emotional charge.

Rehearsing what I should have said. Reconstructing how I had been perceived. Wondering whether I had caused what I was actually reacting to. These loops did not come from nowhere.

They were part of the pattern, too. The mind is trying to restore coherence in situations where coherence had already been broken. The intellect is trying to rescue order from emotional distortion. The self is trying to win certainty where the field itself had been organised around ambiguity.

That is why pattern recognition became liberating.

Not because it removed pain immediately, but because it shifted the level at which I was seeing. Instead of getting trapped only in the latest moment, I could begin recognising the architecture beneath it. I could see that some of what I had been treating as fresh confusion was actually familiar confusion. Old confusion. Repetition wearing new clothes.

And once that happens, something loosens.

Not everything. Not all at once. But something.

The moment no longer has total authority over you, because you are no longer seeing only the moment. You are seeing the shape. You are seeing the wider movement. You are beginning to understand that what feels personal in the immediate sense may also belong to a broader pattern of adaptation, perception, fear, and longing.

That broader seeing gives a person more than information. It gives perspective. And perspective, when grounded enough, begins to return freedom.

It also returns responsibility.

Because once you see the pattern, you can no longer relate to it as innocently as before. You may still struggle with it. You may still get caught in it.

You may still hesitate, soften, doubt, hope, or delay. But some part of you knows now. Some part of you has seen enough to recognise the old shape when it arrives. That recognition is both a gift and a burden. It removes a layer of unconsciousness, but it also removes certain excuses. You can no longer say, *I didn't know.* Now the work changes. It becomes less about discovery and more about embodiment. Less about naming the pattern and more about not surrendering your life to it again.

I think that is why this chapter sits where it does.

Awareness arrived quietly in the previous chapter. Here, that awareness begins to take form. It becomes specific. Relational. Discernible.

It starts tracing the links between past and present, between wound and repetition, between language and destabilisation, between old adaptation and current suffering. It shows that liberation is not only about feeling better. Sometimes it begins by seeing more accurately.

That has certainly been true for me.

Because once I could see the patterns, I began to understand that many of the things I had blamed on personal weakness were actually organised repetitions of earlier pain. I began to understand that some of what I had interpreted as chemistry was familiarity. Some of what I had called patience was self-betrayal.

Some of what I had called complexity was inconsistency repeated often enough to feel normal. Some of what I had called confusion was my body and mind trying to stay coherent inside dynamics that were not coherent at all.

That kind of seeing does not make a person hard. At least, it need not. But it does make them clearer.

And clarity changes what can be tolerated.

If the earlier chapters of Part III begin the shift through awareness, then this chapter deepens that shift by showing what awareness starts to reveal.

Not only the existence of patterns, but their meanings. Not only that they repeat, but how they repeat. Not only where they live in others, but how they have lived in me.

That is where pattern recognition becomes more than observation.

It becomes liberation.

Not total liberation yet. Not final freedom. But the beginning of release from the belief that each pain must be understood only on its own terms.

The beginning of recognising that some of the most important truths in life do not appear once. They appear repeatedly, patiently, painfully, until they are finally seen.

And once seen, they begin to lose the power that unconsciousness once gave them.

Chapter 12 - The Body Knows Before the Mind

Long before I trusted my body, I was already living inside its knowledge.

I just did not recognise it as knowledge.

I recognised discomfort.
I recognised tension.
I recognised agitation, shutdown, confusion, exhaustion, and the strange feeling of knowing something was off before I could explain why.

But I did not yet understand that these were not random disturbances passing through me. Nor did I understand that the body was often perceiving, organising, and responding to reality before the rational mind had formed a coherent sentence about it.

I was still trying to live as though clarity began in thought. What I had to learn, slowly and often painfully, was that much of the time the body already knew what the mind was still trying to debate.

That was not an easy thing to accept.

Partly because I had spent so many years trying to reason my way through experience, and partly because trusting the body can feel dangerous when the body has also been the place where so much pain, overwhelm, and instability have been lived.

When a person has known intense reactions, shutdown, emotional flooding, confusion, or collapse, it can be tempting to distrust the body altogether. To treat it as unreliable. To assume that sensation is a distortion and only thought is to be trusted.

My journey kept teaching me the opposite. The body was not always wrong. Often, it was simply early.

I began to notice this more and more in ordinary moments.

A shift in posture before I had consciously registered discomfort.
A change in breath before I had admitted something felt unsafe.
A heaviness in the chest before I had acknowledged grief.
A restlessness in my system before I had recognised I was forcing myself to remain in an environment that did not feel right.
A subtle tightening around certain people long before they had done anything obvious enough for the rational mind to justify the response.

These were not dramatic moments in themselves. But once noticed, they began to form a pattern. My body was often responding first. Thought was arriving later. Explanation later still.

That did not mean every sensation was a final truth, and I learned to be careful with that distinction. I am not saying every bodily reaction should be obeyed blindly, nor that every discomfort is proof of danger. What I am saying is something more modest and, in my experience, more real: the body registers shifts in the field of experience before the conscious mind has fully organised them. It senses tone, threat, incongruence, pressure, instability, rhythm, safety, and unease in ways that thought often only catches up with afterwards.

The body knows before the mind, not because it is magical, but because it is already participating in reality at a different level.

That was one of the great corrections of my life.

I had spent so long feeling as though I needed to justify what I sensed. To explain it clearly enough before I could trust it. To produce rational evidence for what was happening in me. But the body does not always wait for proof in the way the conscious mind demands it. It responds through sensation. Through tightening.

Through release. Through alertness. Through depletion. Through breath. Through pulse. Through posture. Through the subtle but unmistakable way a nervous system changes when something is safe, unsafe, open, closed, coherent, or contradictory.

Looking back, I can see how often this had been true long before I understood it.

There were relationships where my body never fully settled, even when part of me wanted the story to work. There were environments where I told myself I was fine, yet my body was already braced. There were conversations where my mind was still trying to be reasonable while my body had already begun withdrawing trust. There were social spaces where I felt myself tightening without yet knowing why.

There were other spaces, usually quieter ones, more natural ones, less performative ones, where something in me softened almost immediately, as though my body had recognised a kind of permission my mind was still too distracted to name.

Nature was especially important in that.

I have spoken before about how walking, being outdoors, and stepping away from certain environments brought a kind of calm I did not always understand at the time. What I can see now is that those were not just pleasant habits.

They were relational moments between my body and safety. The change in breath, the easing of pressure, the slowing of mental noise, the sense of being less compressed and more open, all of that was information.

The body was telling me, in its own quiet way, that certain environments nourished coherence while others fed fragmentation.

That mattered more than I knew then, because it began to teach me that peace was not just an abstract ideal. It had texture. It had sensation. It had a bodily signature.

That realisation changed how I understood intuition.

For a long time, intuition felt like a vague or elusive thing, a word people used for something difficult to define. But as my awareness deepened, I began to experience intuition less as a mysterious voice and more as a form of embodied discernment.

Not a dramatic prophecy, not an infallible pronouncement, but a subtle and often immediate knowing carried through the body.

A quiet sense that something fits or does not fit. A recognition that a space is safe enough to exhale in, or unsafe enough to brace against.

A feeling that the words being spoken are not fully matched by the tone carrying them. A physical sense that something in an interaction is off, even while the rational mind is still trying to remain polite, fair, and open.

This was not always easy for me, because my history had taught me to doubt myself in these moments.

To search for reasons not to trust what I was sensing.
To prioritise the appearance of reasonableness over the reality of what was happening inside me.
To stay open longer than was wise.
To explain away the body's unease because I could not yet prove it in language.

But the more I paid attention, the more I noticed that the body's signals, while not always convenient, were often deeply informative. Not infallible, but informative. They were not there to control me. They were there to orient me.

That is an important word here: orient.

The body does not only react. It also orients. It turns towards what feels safe.

It turns away from what feels threatening. It begins opening where there is coherence and closing where there is contradiction. It registers pace, proximity, tone, unpredictability, stillness, noise, warmth, scrutiny, dismissal, and acceptance in ways the conscious mind often underestimates.

Once I began respecting that more, I found I was no longer relating to myself as though I were broken for feeling so much. I was beginning to understand that sensitivity, in the right relationship, can become discernment.

That did not mean I became perfectly calm or endlessly self-trusting overnight. There were still moments of confusion, still moments where the old patterns tried to claim authority, still times when fear and discernment felt close enough to one another that I had to sit quietly and listen more carefully.

Even that was part of the maturing. I was no longer trying to force quick answers. I was learning to stay with what my body was telling me without rushing to condemn it or obey it blindly. I was learning to sense, then reflect, then respond. That sequence was new for me. For much of my life, it had been sensation, reaction, then later reflection. Now another rhythm was slowly becoming possible.

Breath played a large part in that shift.

The breath became one of the clearest places where I could notice my state without immediately getting lost in the story around it. If my breath shortened, if my chest tightened, if I felt compressed or braced, that was not something I needed to moralise.

It was something to notice. Something to honour. Something that told me I was no longer entirely in the present in the way I needed to be. It might mean fear was gathering. It might mean memory had been stirred. It might mean the environment itself was asking too much of my system. But whatever the cause, the breath offered a doorway back into awareness.

Not because breath magically solved everything, but because it brought me into immediate contact with the body's reality instead of the mind's endless argument about that reality.

The heartbeat, too, began to matter differently.

There were times I would feel it rise and, rather than panic about why it was rising, I started learning to ask what in me had already perceived something significant.

Not always danger in the obvious sense. Sometimes pressure. Sometimes overstimulation. Sometimes, emotional significance. Sometimes contradiction. Sometimes simply the old momentum of survival being stirred by familiar conditions.

The heartbeat became less something to fear and more something to listen to.

Posture gave me information as well.

There is a difference between standing open and standing defended. A difference between being physically present and subtly pulling away. A difference between being settled in oneself and being arranged around tension.

Once I started noticing that, I began to understand just how much the body had been communicating my truth even when my words had not yet caught up. The body did not only know before the mind; often, it was already showing what the mind was still trying not to admit.

That recognition became especially important in relation to other people.

For much of my life, I had been highly attentive to the shifts in others — their tone, their posture, their micro-expressions, their energy, the moments where they became tense, evasive, brittle, performative, dismissive, or incongruent. Earlier in life, that sensitivity often overwhelmed me. Later, it became something else.

It became part of how I understood relational truth. Not in a paranoid sense, but in a discerning one. I began to recognise that bodies often tell the truth before words do.

A person may say they are fine, but their body says otherwise. A person may offer reassurance, but something in their posture, tone, or timing reveals distance. A person may present as calm while their nervous system is radiating contraction. None of that makes anyone bad. It simply means the body is participating in communication, whether we admit it or not.

And once I saw that more clearly in others, I had to become more honest about it in myself.

There were times I had stayed in conversations, relationships, or environments long after my body had already withdrawn consent. Long after breath had changed, posture had tightened, intuition had stirred, and the first quiet signs of misalignment had already arrived.

Part of my awakening was learning not to overrule those signals so quickly in the name of politeness, patience, or giving endless benefit of the doubt. Again, not because I wanted to become hardened or suspicious, but because I finally understood that embodied truth must have a place in how I live. Without that, I would always be trying to build a life from the neck up while the rest of me carried a different reality.

That is why this chapter sits where it does.

Chapter 10 marked the beginning of awareness. Chapter 11 deepened that awareness into pattern recognition. This chapter brings the shift into embodiment more fully. It shows that awakening is not only about seeing differently in thought. It is about sensing differently in life. It is about learning to trust what the body has been saying quietly for years. It is about moving from confusion into sensing, from over-intellectualisation into discernment, from trying to think truth into existence to allowing truth to be felt, noticed, and then understood.

I think this is where spiritual coherence starts becoming more real.

Not in abstraction.
Not in grand ideas.
But in the reunion of mind and body.
In the willingness to let sensation inform understanding.
In the humility to admit that the body had often known long before the mind was ready to agree.

That does not reduce awakening to biology, nor does it romanticise the body as infallible. It simply restores the relationship. It makes room for the full human field to participate in truth.

There is something deeply stabilising in that. Because once the body is no longer treated only as a site of pain or a problem to be managed, it begins to become what it had always been capable of becoming: a compass. Not a rigid map.

Not a machine that offers perfect answers. But a living, sensing part of me that can help orient me towards what is coherent, what is safe, what is real, and what is no longer mine to keep arguing with.

If the earlier parts of the book traced how the body carried pain, then this chapter marks a different turn. Here, the body is not only a witness to what has been lived. It is also a participant in what is becoming possible. It is helping guide me back towards myself.

And that matters because the next step in the journey requires something even harder than seeing patterns or trusting sensation.

It requires letting go.

Not only of pain, but of identity.
Not only of old relationships, but of old selves.
Not only of what hurt, but of what once seemed necessary in order to survive.

That is where the shift deepens again.

That is where I must begin letting go of who I was.

Chapter 13 - Letting Go of Who I Was

There is a particular kind of grief that comes when you realise you can no longer continue as the person who once helped you survive.

It is not the grief of losing only other people, though that can be part of it. It is the grief of losing familiarity. Of losing old roles, old identities, old strategies, old ways of being that once made life manageable, even if they also made it smaller.

That grief is difficult because what we must release is not always something we hated. Sometimes we must let go of versions of ourselves that were intelligent, loyal, adaptable, patient, resilient, and deeply committed to trying. The problem is not that those parts were worthless.

The problem is that they were often built in response to pain, and there comes a point when what once protected you begins to prevent you from living more truthfully.

That is the stage this chapter belongs to.

By the time I reached it, something in me had already changed. Awareness had begun to gather. Patterns had become visible. The body had become less of an enemy and more of a guide.

I could no longer pretend I did not know what I knew. But knowing is not the same as releasing. A person can see their old identity clearly and still cling to it. They can know a role no longer fits and still wear it out of habit, fear, loyalty, guilt, or uncertainty. That is what made this chapter so difficult in my own life. I was not only leaving behind pain. I was leaving behind ways of being that had become intertwined with how I understood myself.

Some identities are not chosen in freedom. They are assembled through repetition.

The one who keeps the peace.
The one who explains.
The one who waits.
The one who gives more.
The one who endures.
The one who tries to be understood by everyone.
The one who remains available even when reciprocity has already gone missing.
The one who stays calm on the surface while carrying storms underneath.

These identities do not usually appear all at once. They gather gradually. One accommodation at a time. One compromise at a time. One moment of swallowing what is true to preserve connection.

One moment of stepping away from your own instinct because you are still trying to believe the story in front of you, rather than the feeling inside you.

Over time, those repeated acts become character. They begin to look like who you are. And because they are often reinforced socially, praised as patience, maturity, support, generosity, steadiness, it can take years to realise how much self-abandonment is hidden inside them.

That recognition was sobering for me.

I had to admit that there were parts of my identity I had clung to not because they were fully true, but because they helped me remain acceptable, remain involved, remain needed, remain understandable in the eyes of others.

Validation-seeking can take obvious forms, but it can also take subtler ones. It can look like needing to be perceived as fair. As loyal. As emotionally intelligent.

As someone who always sees nuance.

As someone who gives chances.

As someone who is not bitter, not reactive, not unkind. None of those qualities is wrong in itself.

When they become tied to the need to maintain a version of self that still depends on being received properly by everyone around them, they become trapped. You begin living not only from truth, but from the exhausting effort to ensure that truth is palatable enough to be accepted.

Part of letting go, then, was letting go of the need to be understood by everyone.

That was not easy for me.

Much of my life had been shaped by misunderstanding. Being seen wrongly, interpreted badly, dismissed too quickly, and doubted unfairly. It makes sense, then, that I would develop a strong desire to be understood clearly. But somewhere along the way, that understandable desire became too central. I gave too much of my energy to trying to close the gap between my reality and other people's willingness to meet it.

I wanted the right explanation to land. I wanted sincerity to be recognised as sincerity. I wanted truth to matter enough that if I offered it carefully and honestly, it would at least have a chance of being received. Sometimes it did. But often it did not.

The more I grew, the more I realised that building my life around the hope of universal understanding was keeping me attached to something impossible.

Not everyone will meet you.
Not everyone can hear you.
Not everyone is available to your reality.
Not everyone wants the truth more than they want the comfort of their own interpretation.

That is painful, but it is also freeing.

Because once I accepted that fully, something loosened. I no longer needed to keep arranging myself around the hope that everyone would eventually see me properly if I was only patient enough, articulate enough, open enough, fair enough.

There is a deep exhaustion in living that way. There is also a hidden performance in it. You are still begging, in some quieter emotional form, for permission to exist as you are. Letting go meant refusing that position. Not with arrogance. Not with bitterness. But with a kind of internal dignity I had not always given myself before.

That dignity required grieving old selves.

There was grief in letting go of the version of me who still thought love could be earned through steadiness alone.

Grief in letting go of the version of me who thought explanation would always eventually rescue truth.

Grief in letting go of the version of me who remained too available to those who did not know how to meet availability with care.

Grief in letting go of the version of me who believed that if I stayed calm enough, thoughtful enough, patient enough, things would finally become mutual. It is painful to admit that some of the identities we have inhabited so earnestly were built around hopes that reality never truly agreed to fulfil.

And yet, the grief itself was honest.

Because I was not simply shedding illusions. I was also shedding survival structures. Things that had once carried me. Things that had once made it possible to move through environments, relationships, and emotional fields that I was not yet strong enough to confront differently.

It would be unfair to speak of those older selves with contempt. They were trying. They were doing what they knew. They were formed under conditions that made them necessary.

So this chapter is not about mocking who I once was. It is about blessing him enough to let him rest.

There is a tenderness needed here.

We often speak about growth as though it requires ruthless detachment from the past, but in my experience, it requires something more nuanced than that.

It requires honesty, yes. It requires firmness, yes. But it also requires compassion. Because the self you are outgrowing is usually not your enemy. It is the part of you that got you here. The problem is not that it existed.

The problem is that it cannot take you further than the conditions that created it. At some point, survival identity reaches its limit. It cannot become wholeness simply by trying harder. It must be released.

That release often looks less dramatic than people imagine.

It looked, for me, like no longer chasing closure where closure was never going to come honestly. It looked like stepping out of unhealthy relational loops and refusing to re-enter them simply because they were familiar. It looked like recognising false peace for what it was, not calm, but self-silencing.

It looked like noticing when I was about to explain too much, justify too much, stay too long, soften what should have been clear, or make room for realities that repeatedly invalidated my own. It looked like not forcing a connection where the body had already withdrawn trust. It looked like allowing distance without immediately framing that distance as failure. It looked like realising that letting go is not always the same as giving up. Sometimes it is the first truly faithful act towards your own life.

There was also a particular kind of strength in no longer needing to prove.

For years, so much of my energy had gone into proving things in subtle ways. Proving I was sincere. Proving I cared. Proving I was not the caricature others might have made of me. Proving I could stay composed. Proving I could be fair. Proving I was worth listening to. Proving I was not what the projections around me implied.

That proving takes a tremendous amount of energy, and it rarely ends where you hope it will. Because the more invested people are in misunderstanding you, the less your proof will matter. Eventually, I had to admit that much of this proving was not serving truth. It was serving old pain.

The pain of being unseen. The pain of being doubted. The pain of wanting reality to be shared when it was being defended against instead.

Letting go meant laying that burden down.

It meant accepting that my life could no longer be organised around convincing those who were committed to remaining unconvinced.

It meant trusting that I did not need to keep standing trial in rooms that had already made their decision before I arrived. It meant recognising that truth does not always require endless defence. Sometimes it requires quiet alignment. Quiet departure. Quiet refusal. Quiet clarity.

This is what I mean by acceptance without defeat.

Acceptance is often misunderstood as passivity, as though to accept something is to collapse before it. But that is not the kind of acceptance I am speaking of. I mean accepting what is real without distorting yourself trying to make it something else. Accepting that some relationships are not mutual. Accepting that some people cannot meet you. Accepting that some old roles no longer belong in your life. Accepting that who you were may have been shaped by pain more than you once admitted. Accepting that not every bridge should be rebuilt. Accepting that the life ahead of you cannot be entered honestly while you are still performing an old version of self whose whole structure was built around survival.

There is real power in that kind of acceptance.

Not loud power. Not performative power. But grounded power. The kind that no longer needs to keep arguing with reality in order to feel safe.

The kind that allows grief without letting grief dictate identity. The kind that can say, this was part of me, but it is not all of me.

This protected me once, but it cannot lead me now. This role was adaptive, but it is not my deepest truth.

That is why this chapter is an inner turning point.

Everything before it in Part III has been preparing for this. Awareness arrived. Patterns became visible. The body began to speak as a compass rather than only as a witness. Now the question becomes: what happens when I stop building a life around the structures that those insights have already outgrown?

For me, the answer was not immediate certainty. It was quieter than that. It was a gradual but unmistakable withdrawal of consent from the life I had once been arranging around pain. A refusal to keep performing old selves for the comfort of others. A refusal to mistake being understood by everyone for the condition of being real. A refusal to keep seeking false peace in places that required my diminishment.

And beneath that refusal, something simpler began to appear.

Not a perfected self. Not a grand new identity.
Just less performance.
Less proving. Less begging. Less self-abandonment.

In that reduction, something more essential had room to emerge.

I think that is what letting go truly opened for me. Not emptiness, but room. Room for a self that did not need to be assembled around fear in quite the same way. Room for a life less organised by old misunderstandings. Room for truth to exist without constant justification. Room for dignity. Room for quieter forms of strength. Room for the possibility that who I am is not what I had to become to survive what I once lived through.

If Part II asked what the fracture had been doing inside me, and Part III began showing what became possible once I could finally see it, then this chapter marks the point where seeing becomes release. Not full release, not final freedom, but the first honest letting go of identities that can no longer accompany me where I am going.

And that matters, because the journey cannot continue by insight alone. Eventually, insight must alter the self. It must become lived. It must reshape relationship, language, posture, choice, and presence. It must become the beginning of a return.

That return is not complete yet. But with this chapter, it has begun in earnest.

Part IV - The Return

There is a stage in some journeys where the work stops being only about what has been seen and starts becoming about how that seeing is lived.

That is the return.

Not a return to who you were before the fracture.
Not a return to innocence.
Not a return to the old identities that once held your life together.

It is a return of a different kind. A return to life itself, but from a different centre. A return to relationship, to choice, to ordinary days, to speech, to responsibility, to presence, to the quiet tests that come not in dramatic collapses but in how a person now moves through the world they still inhabit. This is the part of the journey where insight must become embodied in practice. Where awareness must begin to shape how one lives, not only how one reflects.

If Part III was the shift, then Part IV is the integration that follows it.

Not perfection, but steadiness. Not fantasy, but maturity. Not the claim of being healed in some final and polished sense, but the quieter reality of living differently because something real has changed. This section matters because every genuine journey must eventually return to life as it is actually lived. Relationships remain. The body remains. Old patterns may still stir. Difficult days still come. The world does not rearrange itself simply because deeper awareness has arrived. The task, then, is no longer only to see. It is to remain in a relationship with what has been seen without abandoning oneself again.

This is why Part IV must feel grounded, mature, and human.

It is not the part of the book where I pretend to have transcended difficulty. It is the part where I try to tell the truth about what changes when healing becomes less of an idea and more of a lived orientation. When self-awareness becomes a discipline. When discernment becomes quieter and more stable. When boundaries stop being performances of strength and become expressions of care. When peace is no longer confused with numbness or withdrawal, but begins to take shape as a more honest way of inhabiting life.

The chapters that follow bring that return into focus.

Chapter 14 - Living With Awareness, Not Perfection

This chapter begins the return by grounding the journey in integration rather than idealism. It explores humility, daily practice, emotional responsibility, and healing without fantasy. It moves through the reality that there is no final arrival, that difficult moments still arise, but that they can be met differently. This chapter shows that healing is not a polished state. It is a changed relationship to experience, shaped by groundedness rather than performance.

Chapter 15 - Relationships, Language, and Connection

This chapter brings the inner work back into the relational world. It explores communication, authenticity, discernment, boundaries, and the possibility of connection without self-abandonment. It turns towards how I relate differently now, what I no longer tolerate, what real mutuality feels like, and how to speak honestly without aggression. This is where the journey begins to show itself in human relationships, not just in private insight.

Chapter 16 - The Ongoing Journey

This chapter resists the temptation to turn the book into a tidy ending. It explores spiritual growth as continued unfolding, the cycles of clarity and difficulty that remain part of life, and the maturity that comes from accepting incompletion. It moves through the reality that awakening is a process, not an event; that openness must be maintained; that learning continues; and that both pain and progress must be honoured honestly.

Chapter 17 - Traversing the Darkness, Again and Again

This final chapter of the main body returns to the deeper rhythm beneath the whole book: that darkness is not only something faced once, but something encountered in cycles throughout a life. It explores return, resilience, deeper trust, and the soul's ongoing relationship with shadow and truth. It turns towards darkness not as punishment, but as a recurring teacher; towards returning to self repeatedly; and towards living with greater peace rather than greater illusion. This chapter closes the book's main movement with depth, dignity, and openness.

Part IV matters because this is where the journey comes back into real life.

Not life imagined from a distance.
Not life purified of difficulty.
But life as it is: relational, imperfect, recurring, embodied, and unfinished.

This is where the deeper shift must prove itself, not through spectacle, but through ordinary honesty. Through how one responds rather than reacts.

Through the kinds of relationships one now chooses. Through the ability to remain present without collapsing into performance. Through the willingness to keep learning without needing to claim completion.

If Part III asked, *What becomes possible now that I can finally see it?*
Then Part IV asks something more lived:

How do I now carry that seeing into the life that remains?

That is the return.

And it is not the end of the journey.
It is the beginning of living more truthfully.

Chapter 14 - Living With Awareness, Not Perfection

One of the quietest but most important changes in my life was learning that healing does not look like becoming untouchable.

For a long time, I think some part of me imagined that if I did enough work, understood enough, reflected deeply enough, faced enough pain honestly enough, I would eventually arrive at a place where life no longer reached me in the same way. I would be calm. Clear. Resolved. I would no longer find myself caught in old feelings, old sensitivities, old moments of inner conflict. I would become, in some subtle way, beyond the struggle.

But that is not what happened.

What happened was more ordinary than that, and more valuable.

I still have moments. I still feel things deeply. I still notice old patterns stir from time to time. I still encounter situations that touch old places in me. I still know what it is to feel tension, disappointment, grief, frustration, or the first rising signs of an old internal weather. The difference is not that these things have disappeared. The difference is in how I meet them now.

That, I have come to realise, is what healing actually changes.

Not always the fact of experience, but the relationship to it.

In earlier years, I often lived as though every difficult internal movement carried the weight of identity. If I was overwhelmed, it felt as though I was unstable. If I were hurt, it could feel as though I had failed to protect myself. If I shut down, I might interpret that as weakness.

If anger rose, I might judge the whole of myself through that moment. Experience and identity were often too tightly fused. There was very little space between what I was feeling and what I then concluded about myself because I was feeling it.

Now there is more space.

Not always a perfect space. Not endless space. But enough.

Enough to notice an old response beginning without immediately collapsing into it. Enough to say, something is stirring in me, without needing to make that the whole truth of who I am. Enough to feel discomfort without turning it into self-condemnation. Enough to recognise that a difficult moment is not the same as a broken self.

That shift has brought a kind of humility with it.

Because living with awareness is not glamorous. It does not make life clean.

It does not put a person above pain. It does not produce some polished version of the self that moves through the world untouched by old wounds, relational strain, bodily sensitivity, or the ordinary mess of being human. If anything, awareness makes a person more honest about how human they still are. It removes the fantasy that growth means transcendence. It reveals, instead, that growth may look more like responsibility. More like presence. More like refusing to abandon yourself in the moments where life still feels difficult.

That has been one of the greatest lessons for me.

Awareness is not an ornament. It is a discipline.

Not in the harsh sense. Not as punishment. But as a way of living.

It asks something each day. It draws attention. It asks for honesty. It asks that I notice where I am tightening, where I am overriding myself, where I am rushing, and where I am trying to perform calm instead of actually being present.

It asks that I be willing to return, again and again, to what is real in me rather than what looks more acceptable on the surface.

That daily quality matters. Because without it, awareness easily becomes another idea. Another concept I can speak about without fully inhabiting. But life does not ask whether I understand these things in theory. It asks how I meet a difficult conversation.

How I respond when disappointment rises. How I carry myself when tired, triggered, hurt, or uncertain. How do I treat my own inner life when it is not neat? That is where integration becomes visible. Not in insight alone, but in ordinary conduct.

I have found that emotional responsibility sits at the heart of this chapter.

There is a difference between taking responsibility for your inner life and taking blame for everything that touches it. Earlier in life, I often confused the two. I could move too quickly into self-questioning, too quickly into carrying what was not fully mine, too quickly into trying to regulate the whole field around me by modifying myself. But emotional responsibility, as I understand it now, is something steadier than that.

It means being honest about what is mine to work with without collapsing into shame. It means noticing when old patterns are being stirred and choosing not to let them unconsciously organise the whole moment. It means owning my reactions where I need to, tending to my body, honouring my limits, and not using pain as a reason to become careless with others or careless with myself.

That kind of responsibility is not harsh. It is protective.

It has allowed me to stop seeing healing as a state I either possess or fail at, and start seeing it as an ongoing relationship I must keep participating in.

There is no final day on which I wake up and become finished.

There is no perfected version of me waiting just beyond one more insight. There is only this life, this body, this history, this awareness, and the repeated opportunity to meet experience differently than I once did.

That may sound modest, but it has changed my life more than any fantasy of enlightenment ever could.

Because choosing groundedness over performance is not a small thing.

There were many years when I was still, in one way or another, performing. Sometimes for others. Sometimes for myself. Performing resilience. Performing patience. Performing detachment.

Performing understanding. Performing calmly. Not always dishonestly, but not always fully truthfully either. There were times I was trying to appear as though I had made peace with things that I had only learned to suppress.

Times I called something maturity when in truth it was exhaustion. Times I called something balance when in truth it was emotional distance. Times I called something acceptance when in truth it was resignation.

Living with awareness has forced me to become more precise than that.

Groundedness feels different from performance.

It has weight to it.
Less strain.
Less proving.
Less theatre.

Groundedness does not need to advertise itself. It does not rush to reassure others that all is well. It does not make a persona out of being healed. It allows what is true to be true without immediately decorating it.

If I am having a hard moment, groundedness lets that be a hard moment without making it a drama or a personal failure. If I need quiet, it lets quiet be quiet rather than turning it into some elaborate statement. If something hurts, it lets the hurt exist without needing to turn it into identity. There is a dignity that I value deeply now.

I also think this stage of the journey has taught me the importance of rhythm.

Healing, at least as I have lived it, is rhythmic. There are clearer periods and more difficult ones. There are stretches where presence comes more naturally and stretches where life feels heavier, where I have to be more deliberate, more attentive, more protective of my energy, my body, my focus, my boundaries.

The older fantasy of "arrival" had no room for rhythm. It wanted finality. But real life has seasons. And real healing learns how to move with them without constantly concluding that every difficult season means all previous growth was false.

That has been an essential correction for me.

Because there is a particular discouragement that comes when a person expects perfection from their healing. They have one difficult day, one old feeling, one moment of shutdown, one surge of emotion, and suddenly all the old self-judgement returns.

I thought I was past this. I thought I had done the work. I thought I had changed. But the work is not disproved by the return of difficulty. Often it is revealed in how difficulty is now held.

That is the real difference.

I still have moments, but I meet them differently now.

I do not collapse into them quite so quickly.
I do not build my whole identity from them.
I do not hand them total authority.
I do not assume they erase all progress.

Sometimes I pause.
Sometimes I step away.
Sometimes I breathe.
Sometimes I go quiet, but not in the old erased way — more as an act of listening.
Sometimes I recognise that the body needs time before the mind can speak wisely.
Sometimes I simply do less and let that be enough for the day.

This may not sound extraordinary, but in truth, it is the most human form of transformation I know.

Because living with awareness is not about becoming impossible to disturb. It is about becoming less divided when disturbance arrives.

That is what feels different now. I am less at war with my own experience. Less determined to conquer it, deny it, out-think it, or disguise it. More willing to remain in a relationship with it. More willing to ask what is happening rather than only demanding that it stop. More willing to hold both progress and pain in the same life without making them enemies.

There is a softer strength in that.

And perhaps that is what this chapter is really about.

Not strength as force.
Not strength as perfection.
Not strength as appearing unshaken.

But strength is the capacity to remain present, honest, and responsible without pretending to be finished.

That is the return taking root in everyday life.

Not in abstraction. Not in grand spiritual language.
But in the repeated ordinary choice to live with a little more awareness, a little less performance, a little more humility, a little more care.

If Part III was about the shift itself, then this chapter begins to show what that shift looks like when it comes back down into daily living. When awareness becomes less of an insight and more of a way of meeting what arises. When healing stops being imagined as a destination and starts being lived as a relationship. When the person I am becoming no longer needs to be spotless to be real.

That, for me, has been one of the most important forms of peace.

Not the peace of having no more inner movement.
But the peace of no longer needing to pretend that real life should not move me.

And perhaps that is where maturity begins. Not in mastery over experience, but in the ability to stay in an honest relationship with it.

Chapter 15 - Relationships, Language, & Connection

It is one thing to come back to yourself in solitude. It is another thing entirely to remain with yourself in a relationship.

That is where so much of the real work begins to show.

Because relationships do not ask only what you understand about yourself in private. They ask how that understanding lives when another person is present. When tone enters. When timing matters.

When misunderstanding is possible. When affection, frustration, desire, disappointment, projection, expectation, and vulnerability all begin to move between two people at once. It is in that space that discernment either becomes lived or remains only theoretical.

For much of my life, relationships were some of the deepest places of both longing and confusion.

I wanted a connection.
I wanted honesty.
I wanted mutuality.
I wanted to be able to speak and be met, to care and be cared for, to bring truth into the space between myself and another without it becoming a source of tension, dismissal, distortion, or emotional warfare.

But wanting those things and knowing how to live them are not the same.

There were many times in the past when I entered connection carrying old patterns I did not fully understand. I could be open, but too open too quickly.

I could be patient, but in ways that became self-abandonment.

I could explain, but keep explaining long after explanation had ceased to be an act of honesty and had become an act of self-defence.

I could remain available beyond the point where availability was being met with care. I could tell myself I was being fair, calm, loyal, and emotionally mature while quietly staying inside dynamics that were draining, destabilising, or one-sided.

That is not how I want to relate anymore.

One of the clearest signs of change in me has been in how I now understand connection.

Connection is no longer just about closeness. It is about coherence.

It is not enough that someone wants access to me.
It is not enough that there is chemistry, intensity, history, attraction, familiarity, or emotional charge.
It is not enough that words sound good on the surface.

What matters now is whether the connection has integrity in it. Whether there is mutuality. Whether what is spoken matches what is carried. Whether the tone, the posture, the actions, the silences, and the choices all belong to the same truth. Whether I feel more myself in the connection, or less. Whether my body feels permission to settle, or a subtle need to brace.

That change has been profound, because for a long time, I was still orienting towards love through old measures.

Attention.
Need.
Intensity.
Proximity.
Being wanted.
Being missed.
Being pursued.

But those things, on their own, can be deeply misleading. They can mimic connection without containing the steadiness that a real connection requires.

I have learned, sometimes painfully, that being wanted is not the same as being known, and being emotionally entangled is not the same as being met. Real mutuality has a different quality to it. It does not feed on confusion.

It does not require that one person constantly prove, soften, chase, explain, regulate, or accommodate while the other remains inconsistent, defended, or emotionally unavailable. It has reciprocity in it. It has room in it. It has respect in it.

That respect matters more to me now than any intensity ever could.

One of the ways this chapter had to become real in my life was through boundaries.

I used to think boundaries were mainly about saying no. And of course, sometimes they are. But I have come to see that boundaries are not simply refusals. They are structures that protect the conditions in which truth can continue living in you. They are not walls against relationships. They are forms of care that make a healthy relationship possible.

The difficulty, for me, was that I had spent so much of my life adapting around others that clear boundaries could initially feel harsh, selfish, or even guilty.

There was an old pull in me to remain available, to give another chance, to explain more, to avoid disappointing people, to stay open just a little longer in case the shift I was hoping for was still about to happen.

But that old openness had often come at a cost. It had asked me to betray bodily truth in the name of emotional generosity. It had asked me to confuse tolerance with love. It had asked me to make room for dynamics that repeatedly made less and less room for me.

So boundaries began to change in meaning.

They became less about control and more about discernment. Less about pushing people away and more about refusing to keep abandoning myself to maintain the appearance of connection. A boundary could now be something as simple as not continuing a conversation once it had become clear that honesty was no longer being met. It could mean stepping back when tone carried more aggression than openness.

It could mean not over-explaining myself to someone who had already shown they were committed to misunderstanding. It could mean not remaining emotionally exposed in spaces where the field had become subtly unsafe. It could mean allowing distance without turning that distance into self-accusation.

There is a relief in that I did not fully understand until I began living it.

Because real boundaries quiet something in the system. They let the body know it no longer has to endure endlessly to remain loved. They let themselves know it does not have to trade dignity for connection. They let the relationship become something chosen more consciously, not something survived through reflex.

That shift has changed how I speak, too.

Language in relationships matters immensely. Not only what is said, but how it is said, when it is said, why it is said, and from what state it is being spoken from. I know now that honesty is not the same as emotional dumping, and restraint is not the same as dishonesty.

I know that saying what is true does not require aggression, and that a calm tone is not always a sincere one. I know that some words wound because of the charge beneath them, while other words can hold truth firmly without carrying the need to dominate.

This has become important to me because I have known both the pain of not speaking clearly enough and the pain of speaking into spaces that were not able to hold clarity.

What I want now is simpler, though not always easier.

I want to speak honestly without aggression.
I want to remain authentic without forcing.
I want to say what is true without dressing it up so much that it loses its life.
I want to trust my voice without turning it into a weapon.
I want to be able to state where I am, what I feel, what I will and won't accept, and what I need, without collapsing into apology simply for existing as I am.

That has taken practice.

The old patterns do not vanish simply because insight has arrived.

There can still be moments where I feel the urge to say more than is needed, to manage the emotional field too carefully, to protect the other person from the discomfort of my honesty, or to withdraw too quickly because some old part of me still associates expression with friction. But the difference is that I now recognise these impulses as they arise. I can feel when I am beginning to force. I can feel when the explanation is becoming self-protection. I can feel when my voice is about to leave authenticity and enter performance. That awareness has changed the quality of my communication, not by making it perfect, but by making it more conscious.

I think one of the biggest changes has been in what I no longer tolerate.

I no longer tolerate ongoing inconsistency disguised as complexity.
I no longer tolerate projection dressed as intimacy.
I no longer tolerate emotional access without responsibility.
I no longer tolerate being drawn into repeated explanations where there is no shared intention to understand.
I no longer tolerate false peace that requires my silence.
I no longer tolerate the expectation that I should continue making room for realities that repeatedly erase my own.

That does not mean I have become rigid or unkind. Quite the opposite, in some ways. I feel more able now to meet others fairly because I am no longer asking for connection to survive on self-abandonment.

I am less interested in winning. Less interested in proving. Less interested in being right for its own sake. More interested in whether there is enough honesty in the space for something real to grow.

Because real mutuality feels different.

It feels calmer.
Less performative.
Less confusing.
Less charged with hidden agendas.
More spacious.
More consistent.
More respectful of silence.
More capable of holding differences without turning differences into a threat.

Real mutuality does not ask one person to disappear in order for the other to feel secure. It does not require constant translation of one's reality to maintain legitimacy. It does not feed on pressure, guilt, volatility, or endless emotional negotiation.

It allows both people to remain people. It allows speech without coercion. It allows a pause without punishment. It allows truth without immediate collapse.

That has become one of my clearest measures now: can I remain in myself while in connection with you?

If the answer is no, something matters in that.
If I have to shrink, over-explain, brace, soften what I know, manage your reactions, suppress my body's signals, or keep performing steadiness while quietly fragmenting inside, then whatever the connection may be, it is not healthy for me in the deeper sense.

This is not cynicism. It is discernment.

And I think that distinction is important because sometimes people imagine discernment hardens a person. That makes them guarded, distant, severe, and inaccessible. But true discernment, at least as I have come to know it, is not a closing of the heart.

It is the protection of the conditions in which the heart can stay open without being repeatedly violated. It allows softness to survive because it is no longer being asked to live without structure. It allows honesty to remain honest because it is no longer constantly bent around the emotional instability of others. It allows connection to become cleaner, slower, less driven by old hunger and more guided by truth.

That is what this chapter means to me.

It is the point where the inner work returns fully to the human field. Where awareness, pattern recognition, embodiment, and identity release begin to alter the way the relationship itself is lived. Where language becomes more careful. Where connection becomes more honest. Where boundaries become less theatrical and more necessary. Where the self no longer begs for permission to exist in the very spaces it enters.

If Chapter 14 showed that healing is not perfection but a different relationship to experience, then this chapter shows that healing also changes the kind of relationships a person can live in without losing themselves. It shows that inner work is not complete in private reflection alone. It must also be lived between people. In the quality of speech. In the steadiness of presence. In the courage to remain authentic without becoming aggressive, open without becoming naive, and boundaried without becoming cold.

That is no small thing. A relationship is one of the places where old selves are most easily reactivated.

It is also one of the places where new ways of being become most visible. The return, then, is not only to self in solitude. It is to self in connection.

And for that to be real, one final truth must remain in view:

This is still a journey.

There is no final relational mastery waiting just beyond the next lesson. No perfected version of self will never again feel uncertainty, disappointment, tenderness, hope, or the pull of old fears.

There is only the ongoing work of staying awake enough to meet relationships with honesty, dignity, and care.

That is what I now value most.

Not being endlessly understood.
Not being endlessly wanted.
Not being endlessly needed.

But being able to remain true, open, and discerning without leaving myself behind. That is what makes a connection worth having.

Chapter 16 - The Ongoing Journey

There is a temptation, once a person has walked through enough darkness and come into greater clarity, to want the story to settle into something neat.

To believe the work is now done.
To believe the hardest part is behind you.
To believe the journey can finally be arranged into a clean narrative with a clear ending and a stable sense of arrival.

I understand that temptation. There is something deeply human in wanting resolution. In wanting the pain to mean something definite. In wanting the years of confusion, struggle, collapse, reflection, and rebuilding to lead to a place where life no longer feels so unfinished.

But the truth, as I have come to know it, is quieter and less tidy than that.

The journey does not end in the way I once imagined.

It continues.

because nothing changes, but because life itself continues unfolding. New situations emerge. New relationships form. Old wounds may stir in new contexts.

New layers of understanding appear where once there had only been reaction. The self changes, but not into something fixed and completed. It changes into something more able to remain present as life keeps moving.

That has been one of the more humbling lessons for me.

Awakening, as I have lived it, is not an event that permanently lifts a person above the human condition. It is not a final threshold after which pain becomes irrelevant, confusion impossible, or growth unnecessary. It is a process. An unfolding. A continuing relationship with truth, with self, with body, with history, with others, and with the changing conditions of life.

There are clearer seasons and heavier seasons. Periods of integration and periods where something new begins pressing up from beneath the surface, asking to be seen. The work is not finished because the person is not finished. Life keeps calling new things forward. That is not failure. It is simply the nature of being alive.

I think this mattered especially because, earlier in my life, I often longed for completion.

Not in an abstract philosophical sense, but in a lived emotional one. I wanted to feel done with certain forms of pain. Done with certain loops. Done with the repeated need to revisit old themes, old sensitivities, old relational patterns.

There was a part of me that believed if I learned deeply enough, felt honestly enough, and worked hard enough on myself, I would eventually reach a point where the old terrain would no longer return.

What I know now is more realistic, and in some ways more compassionate.

The terrain may return.
But I do not return to it as the same person.

That is the difference.

There are still moments where something old stirs in me. A familiar tension. A sudden heaviness. A subtle bracing in the body. A memory thread that links the present to something earlier. But those moments no longer carry the same authority they once did.

They no longer define the whole field. They no longer drag me so automatically into the same conclusions. The old movement may still pass through, but I meet it from a different place now. A more aware place. A less fused place. A place with more room in it.

That does not make life static. It makes it honest.

Because honesty leaves room for cycles.

There are cycles of clarity and cycles of difficulty. Cycles of feeling more integrated and cycles where life reveals some remaining edge of self that still needs tenderness, attention, or truth.

The problem is not that these cycles exist. The problem begins only when we interpret them badly, when we assume that the return of difficulty means all previous growth was false, or when we turn normal human recurrence into evidence that we are failing at healing.

I have had to learn not to do that.

There have been times when I felt steadier, more grounded, more inwardly coherent, and then something in life would happen and I would feel an older ache move again. In earlier years, I might have met that with discouragement or shame. I might have thought, *why is this still here?* Or *I should be past this by now.* But maturity, I think, has less to do with eradicating recurrence and more to do with not collapsing into those old judgements every time life becomes difficult again.

Maturity means allowing life to remain alive.

It means accepting that growth does not erase complexity. It deepens our relationship to it. It means understanding that healing is not disproved by struggle, and awareness is not invalidated by the return of pain.

It means remaining open to the fact that each new phase of life may ask something different of us. Something we did not need in the last phase. Some strength, honesty, or surrender that could only emerge now because we have become capable of bearing it.

That has required openness from me.

Not the old openness that left me too exposed to everyone and everything, but a more grounded openness. An openness to learning. To correct. To see that my current understanding, however hard-won, is still not the whole of reality. An openness to the fact that I can be clear in one area of life and still blind in another. That I can have grown greatly and still have more to learn. That there may be further layers of self, of history, of embodiment, of relationship, and of spiritual depth that I have not yet fully met.

That kind of openness is not a weakness.

It is a reverence for the fact that life exceeds any image I have of being "finished."

I think this is one of the reasons the journey has become more peaceful for me over time, not because I have fewer questions, but because I no longer expect life to become simple in order for me to trust it. I no longer require total resolution before I allow myself some ease.

I no longer measure the truth of my growth only by whether difficulty returns. I measure it more by how I now meet that difficulty. With more patience. More awareness. More dignity. More willingness to stay with what is true without needing to dramatise it or outrun it.

There is a kind of softness in that, though not a passive one.

A softer relationship to incompletion.

Earlier in life, incompletion often felt threatening. It suggested uncertainty, instability, lack, and unresolved things.

Now I understand incompletion differently. Not as failure, but as a condition. We are unfinished because we are alive.

There is still life ahead of us, still relationships, still change, still death, still love, still loss, still seasons of insight, still seasons of fatigue, still things in us that have not yet been asked to come forward. That is not something to be solved. It is something to be respected.

To accept incompletion is not to lower the standard of one's life. It is to stop trying to force life into a static image of what healing ought to look like.

It is to allow both pain and progress to coexist honestly.

This matters to me because I do not want this book, or my own life, to become one more polished account that gives the impression of final arrival. That would not be truthful. I have come through a great deal. I have learned much. I have changed deeply.

I trust myself, my body, and my discernment more than I once did. I no longer live in quite the same unconscious ways. I no longer organise my life around some of the old wounds in the same way. I have found forms of peace, stability, and honesty that I value profoundly.

And still, the journey continues.

There are still things to learn. Still deeper levels of surrender. Still moments where life reveals some remaining attachment, some subtle old fear, some inherited echo, some place in me that must become more honest, more embodied, more aligned. I do not say that with despair. I say it with respect. Because this ongoingness is not only a burden. It is also a possibility.

It means life is still speaking.
It means the soul is not yet done unfolding.
It means awareness still has further to travel in daily life.
It means there are still forms of love, truth, and presence I may yet grow into.

That is not something I want to resist anymore.

If anything, this chapter marks a deepening of trust.

Not trust that life will spare me difficulty.
Not trust that I will never feel old pain again.
Do not trust that clarity will remain constant without effort.

But trust that I can continue.

Trust that I can meet what returns differently.
Trust that difficult seasons do not cancel the deeper truth.
Trust that the journey does not have to be complete in order to be meaningful.
Trust that I can remain a student of my own life without becoming lost in it.
Trust that pain and progress can both belong to a mature spiritual life.

This is why I see awakening now less as an escape and more as a way of participating differently.

More honestly.
More consciously.

More gently.

More responsibly.

More openly.

The ongoing journey is not an inconvenience added after the "real work" is done. It is the real work, lived over time. It is what keeps insight from becoming rigid. It is what keeps growth from becoming performance. It is what prevents the self from hardening around its latest version of the truth and calling that completion.

And perhaps that is a deeper form of peace than I once imagined.

Not the peace of having ended the journey.
But the peace of no longer needing to pretend that it should end in order to be worthwhile.

If this chapter does one thing, I hope it restores dignity to the unfinished life. To the person who has grown deeply and still has more to learn. To the person who has come far and still has moments of difficulty. To the person who can honour both what has healed and what still asks for care. That is not a contradiction. That is maturity.

Part IV began by returning the journey to real life. This chapter makes clear that real life does not offer tidy endings. It offers rhythm. It offers recurrence. It offers continued unfolding. And the more honestly I have accepted that, the less pressure I have felt to become some perfected version of myself in order to justify all that I have lived through.

I do not need to be finished to be faithful to the journey.

I only need to remain willing.

Willing to see.
Willing to learn.
Willing to return.
Willing to live the truth I have already found, while staying open to truths I have not yet fully met.

That is where this chapter leaves me.

Not complete.
But more at peace with incompletion.

And in some ways, that may be one of the clearest signs that something real has changed.

Chapter 17 - Traversing the Darkness, Again & Again

There is a quiet truth that only begins to reveal itself once a person has walked far enough through their own experience. The darkness does not end, not in the way we once hoped it would. It changes, it softens in places, it becomes more familiar and less overwhelming, but it does not disappear entirely.

It was never only something outside of us to begin with. It was part of the terrain, part of the movement, part of the unfolding, and as long as life continues, that unfolding continues with it.

What changes is not that darkness vanishes, but that we no longer meet it in the same way. There was a time when darkness felt like something that consumed me, something I had to escape, fix, outrun, or understand completely before I could feel safe. It carried weight, confusion, and intensity, often leaving me with the sense that I was either inside it or free from it, with very little space in between.

Now I see something else. Darkness returns, but differently. It may arrive as a familiar feeling in the body, a subtle contraction, a quiet unease, or a memory that carries emotion with it.

It may come as a moment of disorientation or a question that does not resolve immediately. But it no longer holds the same authority it once did. It no longer defines the entire field of experience. There is space around it now. Awareness moves alongside it, and because of that, it becomes something I can meet rather than something I am entirely lost inside.

This is what the journey has changed. Not life itself, but my relationship to it. And perhaps this is why the title of this book carries more than it first appears to. Traversing the darkness is not something that happens once. It is something that happens again and again, not as punishment or failure, but as part of being alive.

Across cultures, philosophies, and spiritual traditions, this pattern appears in different forms. Some speak of cycles, some of death and rebirth, some of descent and return. There are those who describe it as the hero's journey, others as the night of the soul, and others still as the gradual unwinding of illusion.

Even in more sceptical perspectives, where spiritual language is set aside, there is still recognition of recurrence within the human psyche. Emotional patterns return, behaviours repeat, and certain forms of suffering reappear until they are seen more clearly. The language may differ, but the underlying movement remains the same. We return, again and again, but we do not return as the same person.

This is where something deeper begins to take shape. Resilience, as I once understood it, was about becoming strong enough to withstand life.

Now I see it differently. Resilience is not hardness, not numbing, and not detachment from feeling. It is the ability to remain present, even when something familiar and difficult arises. It is the capacity to feel without collapsing, to observe without immediately reacting, and to stay with what is true without needing to distort it or escape it. It is a quieter strength, one that allows life to move through you without requiring you to shut down to survive it.

There are moments in life that do not fit neatly into explanation, moments that stand apart not because they resolve everything, but because they open something that cannot easily be closed again. There was one such moment for me. I was sitting with a friend.

He had just finished work, and we were catching up, laughing and joking in a relaxed, easy atmosphere. At one point, I rested my arm on my leg and brought my hand up to my chin. I remember feeling briefly meditative, so I closed my eyes.

Then, suddenly, my entire visual field went white. It seemed to come from the left at an angle, as though something was entering my head. At the same time, I felt a surge of energy, warmth, and a deep sense of relaxation. I had a visual of my brain rising out of my head. It appeared red, and I remember a sensation that felt like a shift in awareness rather than physically leaving my body. As the brain rose, I saw the hemispheres fusing. I did not panic. I did not try to stop it. I was simply in it.

Then I heard voices. It felt like more than one, though it was difficult to distinguish clearly. What stood out was that it did not feel like a memory. It did not feel like something being replayed. It felt present, calm, and controlled. They said, "Don't worry. This is your destiny. You will ascend this lifetime. Follow your path."

And then it ended.

I came back as if waking from something I could not fully explain. I became emotional and began to cry, but these were not tears of fear. My friend looked concerned and asked what was wrong.

I told him I was okay and that I couldn't really explain what had just happened, but that I hoped one day he might experience something like it himself. To me, it felt like almost no time had passed, but he told me I had been unresponsive for around thirty to forty seconds, which had worried him.

From that moment on, things began to change. At first, there was a sense of detachment from others, and I felt unsure about what I had experienced. I reached out to speak to people. Some listened, and others ignored me. I felt a deepening within myself that I had not known before. I began to notice things differently, to see patterns, to have realisations that had not been available to me previously.

I also experienced periods of isolation. The more I shared what I was going through, the more I encountered misunderstandings. Some people suggested I was delusional. Others dismissed what I was saying entirely. There were moments where I questioned myself, moments where I felt alone in what I was trying to understand.

I went to the doctor. He listened carefully, carried out checks, and told me he believed everything was okay. He said it sounded like I had experienced an epiphany. That did not explain the experience fully, but it gave me enough grounding to continue without fear that something was physically wrong.

From there, my work began. I started to learn about what I had experienced, to research, to reflect, and to share where I could. I had visions, ideas, and a growing sense of direction, but I also learned quickly that sharing these things did not always bring connection. In many cases, it brought distance.

Over time, I stopped trying to define the experience in absolute terms. I do not know for certain whether it was something neurological, psychological, spiritual, or something that does not fit neatly into any single framework. I do not know whether it was an experience of God, something beyond current understanding, or simply a state the brain can enter under certain conditions.

I no longer feel the need to decide.

Because this was never about proving a point.

It is simply the honest sharing of what I experienced, what I learned from it, and how it shaped the way I began to move through life. That moment did not give me answers. It changed my direction. It deepened my attention and brought me into a process that has been ongoing ever since. That process has not been easy. It has included confusion, intensity, growth, questioning, and periods where I had to learn how to remain grounded while exploring something I could not fully explain.

But through all of that, something else developed. Not certainty, but trust. A deeper trust in the process itself, rather than in any fixed explanation of it.

This is where the chapter returns to its core. The journey is ongoing. There was no final arrival in that moment, no completion, no transformation into something beyond being human. There was a shift, and from that shift, a path unfolded. A path that has included difficulty, growth, connection, isolation, learning, unlearning, and returning. Returning again and again.

Spiritual life, as I have come to understand it, is not about escaping darkness. It is not about rising above the human experience or becoming something untouched by it. It is about becoming more honest within it, more present, more able to see clearly without needing to distort what is seen. It is about being able to feel without being consumed, and to live without needing life to conform to an idea of what it should be.

This is why I no longer see darkness as something to eliminate. It is something that returns, but each time it returns, there is an opportunity to meet it differently. To remain with yourself. Do not abandon your own experience. To not turn away from what is difficult simply because it is difficult, and to not create an illusion to avoid truth. But also, not to exaggerate suffering where space now exists.

There is more peace now, not because life is easier, but because I no longer resist it in the same way. There is less need to prove, less need to control, and less need to be understood by everyone. There is more space to simply be present, to experience, to move, and to return.

Returning to the body. Returning to awareness. Returning to honesty. Returning to self.

There is no final place where this becomes unnecessary. There is only a growing familiarity with the path and a deeper trust in your ability to walk it. Meaning does not come from reaching an endpoint. It comes from how you move through what is in front of you.

I am grateful to experience life and to be present within it. My vision, my aims, and my goals were never about becoming something above others or proving something to the world.

They were about coming back to myself, about feeling more at peace within my own experience, and about creating something that might allow others to recognise something within themselves. Not to follow me, not to agree with me, but to relate more honestly to their own lives, and perhaps, in doing so, relate more honestly to others.

This is not a message of proving a point. It is not about whether others are right or wrong, or whether I am more spiritual or less spiritual than anyone else. It is simply the return to myself. I am not perfect. This journey is ongoing. There was no clear beginning, no fixed middle, and there is no final destination, only the experience of being.

I am who I identify as, James Miller, and this is the flow of my experience. I exist beyond my thoughts, beyond my feelings, and beyond my beliefs, and yet I live through them. I am present, for myself, and for you.

If there is anything this chapter leaves behind, it is this. You will traverse the darkness more than once, but you will not be the same person each time you do. And in that, there is something quietly profound.

Not because it removes the difficulty of life, but because it reveals something deeper within it. Something that remains. Something that returns. Something that continues.

Again and again.

Final Reflection & Integration

If you have reached this point in the book, then you have already travelled through memory, fracture, silence, grief, confusion, awakening, return, and the quieter forms of truth that take time to recognise.

You have moved through the inner architecture of pain, the ways a self is shaped before it can defend itself, the ways the body holds what the mind cannot yet name, and the long, uneven work of coming back into relationship with what is real. It would be easy, at the end of such a journey, to want a neat conclusion. A summary. A final answer. A statement that ties everything together and closes the door gently behind you.

But real life rarely works that way.

The end of a book is not the end of a life. Understanding something is not the same as living from it. Recognition does not instantly become embodiment. A truth may be seen clearly in one season and then tested again in another.

That is why this final section matters. It is not here to provide a polished ending or to offer some final formula for healing. It is here to create space. Space to pause. Space to reflect. Space to allow what you have read to become something more than thought.

Space to notice what has stirred in you, what has resisted, what has softened, and what may now be asking for your attention more honestly than before.

Reflection, if done well, is not performance. It is not the art of sounding deep. It is the willingness to remain with yourself long enough for something true to come forward. Integration is not the act of becoming perfect.

It is the quieter process of allowing what you have seen to begin changing how you relate to yourself, your body, your history, and the people around you. That process cannot be rushed. It cannot be forced. It can only be entered.

So what follows is not a test and not a prescription. It is an invitation. An invitation to meet yourself more directly. To let certain questions stay open. To let certain truths deepen without immediately trying to solve them. To return, in your own way, to the places within you that may still be waiting for language, witness, honesty, or care.

One of the great difficulties in healing is that pain often becomes identity before it becomes understanding. A person does not simply suffer; they begin to believe they *are* the thing that formed around the suffering.

They become the quiet one, the difficult one, the overly sensitive one, the one who always has to explain, the one who keeps the peace, the one who overgives, the one who shuts down, the one who performs strength while quietly fragmenting inside.

Over time, these roles can feel more real than the self beneath them. So part of reflection is not simply asking what happened to you, but asking what you came to believe about yourself because of what happened.

That is not a small distinction.

Many people can remember pain in fragments. Fewer can recognise the inner conclusions that pain quietly taught them. That they are too much. Not enough. Hard to love. Safer silent. Valuable only when useful. Acceptable only when regulated, accommodating, helpful, or easy to manage.

These are not merely thoughts. They become embodied positions. They become ways of entering rooms, relationships, conversations, and even solitude. And unless they are brought into awareness, they continue shaping life long after the original conditions have changed.

So pause, for a moment, and ask yourself this with more honesty than urgency: what pain have I mistaken for identity? Not what pain have you suffered, but what pain have you taken into the structure of self?

Where have you confused adaptation with truth?

Where have you mistaken what you had to become to survive for who you most deeply are?

Sit with that question slowly. Do not rush to answer it well. Let it move around your body as much as your thoughts. Notice whether some answers come immediately because they are well-rehearsed, and whether others arrive more quietly, perhaps with discomfort, with sadness, or with a strange kind of relief. Often, the answers that matter most are the ones that loosen something in the chest as they are admitted.

You may find it helpful to write from different voices within yourself.

Write first from the part of you that adapted. Let that part explain what it had to do, what it had to believe, what it had to suppress, and why.

Then write from the part of you now reading this, the part that has greater awareness, greater honesty, greater distance.

Let that part answer with compassion rather than contempt. Not with, "You were wrong," but with, "I understand why you became this way, and I also know you do not have to live there forever." There is something powerful in allowing these inner positions to meet each other without violence.

Another central question of this book has been the question of silence. Not silence in the abstract, but the many forms it takes. The silence of protection. The silence of fear. The silence of overwhelm. The silence of not being believed often enough. The silence of learning that truth may cost too much in certain environments.

Silence can also become something else. It can become discernment. It can become a pause that protects life rather than represses it. It can become the place where deeper truth begins to gather.

So ask yourself: where are you still silencing yourself?

Be precise. Is it in a relationship? In your family? In your work? In your creative life? In your body? In your spiritual life? In the language, you do not let yourself use? In the boundaries you know you need but still soften too quickly? In the questions you are afraid to ask, because the answer may require change? Or perhaps more subtly, in the way you edit what you feel before it even reaches your own awareness?

There are forms of self-silencing so normalised that they no longer feel like silencing at all. Laughing off what hurts. Explaining away discomfort. Remaining available after trust has quietly gone. Over-intellectualising what the body already knows.

Calling something peace when it is actually self-erasure. If you want to work with this honestly, write down three recent moments where you said less than was true. Then ask why. What were you protecting? What were you afraid would happen if you spoke more clearly? What old cost did your body remember before your mind even had time to explain itself?

Do not use this as a way of accusing yourself. Use it as a way of understanding the conditions under which your voice disappears. Because the goal is not to become loud. The goal is to become honest enough that your inner life no longer has to split itself so dramatically in order to survive contact with the world.

This brings us to the body, which has moved through the entire manuscript as witness, memory, and guide. One of the most important practices of integration is to stop treating the body as background. Most people spend years trying to interpret life only through thought, while the body has already been telling the truth in sensation, breath, posture, contraction, agitation, numbness, warmth, openness, fatigue, or unease. To integrate what you have read, you must begin asking not only, "What do I think?" but also, " What does safety feel like in my body?

This question matters because many people know what danger feels like far more quickly than they know what safety feels like. Danger is loud. Safety can be subtle. Especially if your system was formed in inconsistency, criticism, emotional volatility, or environments where you had to stay alert, safety may feel unfamiliar at first. It may not feel euphoric. It may feel quiet. Ordinary. Spacious. Less charged. Less performative. More like an exhale than a revelation.

So begin small. Think of a place, person, environment, or activity where your body feels less defended. Not perfect, not healed, not blissful, simply less defended.

What changes there?

Does your breath deepen?

Do your shoulders soften?

Does your jaw unclench?

Does your mind become less noisy?

Do you feel less need to explain yourself?

Less need to perform? Do you need to monitor the emotional field around you? These are not minor details. They are part of your body's vocabulary of safety.

Try writing a page that begins with the sentence: Safety in my body feels like... Let yourself continue without over-editing. You may discover that the answer is not only about calm, but about permission. Permission to take up space. To not anticipate an attack.

To not explain your presence. To not be managing everyone else's emotional weather at the same time. Once you know more clearly what safety feels like, you are less likely to confuse intensity for intimacy or numbness for peace.

From there, another question opens naturally: what are you ready to see clearly?

Not what sounds noble to say. Not what you think you *should* be ready for. What are you actually ready to see? Perhaps you are ready to see that a relationship you called complex has long been harmful. Perhaps you are ready to see that your need to be understood by everyone has become a way of organising your life around people who are not available to reality.

Perhaps you are ready to see that you are more tired than you admit. Or that your identity still depends on being needed. Or that your calm is sometimes still suppression. Or that your spiritual language occasionally protects you from ordinary human grief.

Clarity often begins where the excuse begins to weaken. So write two columns. On one side, list the stories you keep telling about a difficult area of your life. On the other side, list what may also be true if you stop protecting the story. Not what is dramatically true.

Not what is cruelly true. Just what is quietly, stubbornly true when you stop decorating the situation to make it easier to keep?

This kind of exercise can be uncomfortable, but discomfort is not always a sign of harm. Sometimes it is simply the feeling of a self-image loosening.

Another central theme of this final section is voice, not only your adult voice, but the younger parts of you that still live beneath present choices.

So ask yourself: what version of you is asking to be heard?

Is it the child who was not believed?

The adolescent who learned to mask?

The adult who has become tired of over-functioning?

The part of you that still wants someone to say, "You were right to feel what you felt"?

The part that wants rest?

The part that wants dignity?

The part that no longer wants to keep proving?

The part that still carries grief has not been permitted to name?

You might try writing a dialogue here as well. Let that version of you speak in plain language. No theory. No polish. Then let your current self answer.

The point is not to fix the younger part immediately, but to stop leaving them in isolation. Integration often begins when parts of the self that have long been exiled are allowed back into a relationship with the whole.

There is also a relational dimension to this work that cannot be ignored. Much of what has wounded people happened in relationships, and so much of what heals them must eventually return there, too.

Not necessarily through reconciliation with everyone, but through a more honest relationship to connection itself. So reflect on this: where in your life are you still confusing familiarity with love?

Where are you confusing being needed with being cherished?

Where are you still over-explaining in the hope that explanation will rescue you from another person's unwillingness to see?

Where are you mistaking your endurance for your depth?

If it helps, think of three relationships: one that drains you, one that confuses you, and one that steadies you. Write honestly about what each relationship asks of your body, your language, your boundaries, and your sense of self. Who do you become in each?

Where do you feel more like yourself, and where do you feel arranged around the needs, moods, or perceptions of another?

Integration is not only inner. It changes what kinds of relationships your system can tolerate without cost.

It is also worth reflecting on anger, because many people on this kind of journey either fear it too much or romanticise it too quickly. Anger, in its healthier form, is often the body's refusal to keep absorbing what should not continue. But if anger is constantly suppressed, it may harden into resentment or leak out as self-attack.

If it is constantly indulged, it may become another form of blindness. So ask:

What does my anger know that my polite self has been trying not to admit?

What boundary, grief, betrayal, or truth sits beneath it? And how can I listen to that without becoming ruled by it?

Then there is grief. Not only grief for what happened, but grief for what did not happen. The care you did not receive. The attunement that never came.

The years spent adapting. The relationships that could not become what they claimed they were.

The selves you had to become too early. Grief is often the hidden companion of awakening, because seeing more clearly also means mourning more honestly. So give grief a place here. Write not only about what hurt, but about what was absent. Sometimes that is where the deeper wound lives.

You may also want to reflect on your spiritual life, if that language belongs to you. Ask whether your spirituality has made you more honest or merely more articulate.

Has it brought you closer to your body, your truth, your relationships, your limits, your humility? Or has it occasionally become another way of explaining away pain too quickly?

Spiritual life, if it is real, should deepen contact with reality, not weaken it. It should make you less performative, not more. Less inflated, less certain, less obsessed with proving, and more willing to sit in mystery without abandoning the human.

A gentle integration practice that may help here is this: at the end of a day, instead of asking, "Did I do well?" ask three quieter questions.

Where did I remain with myself today?

Where did I leave myself?

What helped me return?

This is a simple discipline, but over time, it teaches a different kind of self-awareness. Less judgement. More relationships. Less performance. More truth.

Another useful practice is to build your own language of return. Write down five things that help bring you back when you begin to drift into overwhelm, over-explanation, self-silencing, or old relational loops. They might be concrete: walking, cold air, stillness, music, prayer, writing, stepping away from a conversation, noticing your breath, placing a hand on your chest, sitting near trees, making tea slowly, turning your phone off, resting your eyes. The point is not to create a perfect ritual. It is to recognise that return is not only a concept. It requires conditions.

You may also want to create a page titled: What I know now. On it, write the truths you do not want to lose when life becomes noisy again. They might be things like: My body often knows before my mind.

Not everyone will meet me. Silence is not always peace. Attention is not always love. I do not have to keep proving. A difficult moment is not the same as a broken self. Safety feels quieter than intensity. Returning is part of the journey. Truth does not need theatricality. Keep the page. Read it when the old weather returns.

And perhaps most importantly, allow yourself to remain unfinished.

There is dignity in a life that is still learning. There is no need to make a final identity out of your healing, your wounding, your awakening, or your insight. Let the work stay alive. Let it continue maturing. Let yourself remain teachable without becoming ungrounded. Let what is true today be true today, without demanding that it become the last word on who you are.

If this book has carried any central thread, perhaps it is this: healing does not begin when life becomes easy. It begins when we stop abandoning what is real inside us. And integration, in turn, deepens when we stop expecting ourselves to become perfect in order to deserve peace.

So take your time here. Return to these questions slowly. Write, rest, revisit.

Let your answers change.

Let your body answer where language cannot yet.

Let the younger selves in you speak.

Let the wiser self answer with steadiness, not superiority.

Let truth be truth without making it a performance.

Let peace be quieter than the image. Let your life remain human.

When you are ready, continue.

Not as someone who has finished the journey, but as someone who now knows how to return.

Acknowledgements

This book would not exist without the many experiences, tensions, losses, questions, and moments of grace that shaped it. Some of those moments were painful. Some were confusing. Some were beautiful. Many were difficult to understand while I was living through them. But each, in its own way, helped form the path that led here.

I want first to acknowledge the people who have been part of my life, both those who supported me directly and those whose presence, actions, absences, or misunderstandings shaped me in ways I only came to understand much later.

Not every influence in a life feels positive while it is happening, but even the more difficult parts of our history can become part of what deepens us, if we are willing to meet them honestly enough.

To my family, thank you for the love that existed alongside the complexity. Thank you for the care that was given, even where understanding was sometimes incomplete. Our lives are rarely neat, and families rarely carry only one kind of truth.

This book was written in the spirit of honesty, but also with the recognition that love and difficulty often coexist, and that understanding can deepen long after childhood has ended.

To the friends, listeners, and readers who have engaged with my work over the years, thank you. Some of you have listened quietly. Some have reached out. Some have shared their own experiences with great openness. All of that matters. There is something profoundly meaningful about discovering that what once felt isolating in private can become a point of recognition between people.

I also want to acknowledge those who have felt misunderstood, unseen, silenced, or inwardly divided. Those who have questioned themselves because the world around them could not meet their experience with clarity.

Those who have carried more than others have realised. Those who have continued, even without neat explanations. This book is for you as much as it is from me.

My wider body of work has also shaped this book. Across each project, I have been circling many of the same core concerns from different angles: perception, language, trauma, identity, the nervous system, consciousness, influence, self-awareness, and what it means to come back into a truthful relationship with oneself. In that sense, this book does not stand alone.

It belongs to a longer inquiry, one that has taken form through years of reflection, study, writing, and lived experience.

So I also want to acknowledge the path itself. The questions that did not let go.

The experiences that could not be neatly explained. The moments of collapse that later became moments of clarity. The silence that became a place of listening. The darkness that, over time, became not only something to survive, but something to walk through with more honesty and less fear.

Finally, thank you to life itself. Not because it has been easy, but because it has been real. And because, through everything, it continued to offer the possibility of return.

About the Author

James Miller is an independent writer, researcher, and creator whose work explores the meeting point between human experience, awareness, language, the nervous system, identity, and perception. His writing is grounded in lived experience while also drawing from psychology, philosophy, systems thinking, trauma awareness, spirituality, and reflective self-inquiry.

Across his books and wider body of work, James has developed a voice that is both personal and observational, combining inner truth with broader reflection on how people are shaped by family, culture, institutions, emotional history, and unseen patterns of conditioning.

His work often returns to recurring themes: misunderstanding, self-abandonment, embodiment, discernment, healing, and the long, uneven process of becoming more honest with oneself.

He is the author of:

- The Inversiverse - Waking Up In A World Built To Keep You Asleep

- My Inner Child Was Broken

- The Resonance Matrix - The Anatomy of Influence & The Linguistic Somatic Decode

- The Consciousness Code - How Awareness, Language and the Nervous System Shape Human Behaviour

- If the brain were an App, Would You Use It?
- Traversing the Darkness - A Spiritual Journey

His work is not intended as doctrine, but as an invitation to deeper reflection.

Rather than offering fixed answers, James writes to create space for recognition, the kind that helps people relate more honestly to themselves, to one another, and to the deeper patterns shaping their lives.

About This Place Called Earth

This Place Called Earth is the wider creative and reflective home for James Miller's body of work.

It exists as a space for inquiry into what it means to be human in a world shaped by language, conditioning, influence, memory, culture, trauma, consciousness, perception, and the nervous system.

Rather than presenting one rigid ideology or fixed doctrine, This Place Called Earth brings together a range of books, podcasts, presentations, and ongoing series that explore these themes from different angles.

At its heart, the work is concerned with relationships: the relationship between body and mind, between self and world, between language and meaning, between conditioning and identity, between survival and truth.

Some projects lean more psychological, some more philosophical, some more spiritual, and some more cultural or systemic.

What connects them is a shared intention: to help make visible what often remains hidden beneath ordinary life.

Beyond the books, This Place Called Earth includes several ongoing podcasts and presentation series that approach related themes through different forms of discussion, reflection, and analysis.

These include:

- The Inversiverse

- The Unfiltered Human on the Fringe

- The Body Knows

- The Linguaverse

- The Shadow Spectrum

- Mirror Talk: The Language of the Nervous System

- Moral & Ethical Inversions

- Somatic Inversions

- Invisible Hands

- The Resonance Matrix

- The Consciousness Code Podcast

Together, these projects form a wider body of work exploring awareness, embodied meaning, healing, shadow work, identity, manipulation, language, regulation, and the subtle processes that shape human behaviour. All current series, playlists, and presentation hubs are linked through the main site and YouTube channel.

This Place Called Earth is not about offering final answers. It is about creating space for deeper questions, deeper attention, and a more conscious relationship with the forces that shape human life from within and without.

Suggested Reading

The following books may be helpful for readers who want to continue exploring themes related to trauma, identity, nervous-system awareness, perception, spirituality, healing, and human behaviour.

Other writers and thinkers

Gabor Maté - for work on trauma, stress, addiction, and the long-term effects of emotional disconnection.

Bessel van der Kolk - for insight into how the body stores trauma and why healing is not only cognitive.

Alice Miller - for her writing on childhood wounding, emotional repression, and the hidden legacy of early pain.

Carl Jung - for foundational work on shadow, individuation, symbolism, and the deeper layers of the psyche.

John Bowlby - for understanding attachment, separation, and the shaping power of early relational experience.

Peter Levine - for body-based approaches to trauma and nervous-system regulation.

Donald Winnicott - for ideas around the true self, false self, emotional development, and relational holding.

Irvin D. Yalom - for existential reflections on fear, meaning, isolation, death, and the human condition.

Viktor E. Frankl - for his work on meaning, suffering, responsibility, and spiritual endurance.

Michael A. Singer - for reflections on inner observation, surrender, and the movement beyond identification with thought.

Thomas Moore - for soulful reflections on depth, the inner life, and the importance of tending to what modern culture often neglects.

Clarissa Pinkola Estés - for mythic, symbolic, and archetypal approaches to instinct, psyche, and soul.

Eckhart Tolle - for writing on presence, identification, and the psychological weight of unconscious thought.

James Hillman - for a more imaginal and soul-centred approach to psyche, meaning, and human depth.

A note on reading

Not every reader will resonate with every perspective. Some approaches are clinical, some philosophical, some spiritual, and some more sceptical or evidence-based.

That is part of the value. No single framework holds the whole of human experience. The aim is not to agree with everything, but to deepen inquiry, reflection, and one's own relationship with truth.

Disclaimer

This book is intended for **educational and informational purposes only**. It reflects the author's personal experiences, perspectives, and independent inquiry, and is not a substitute for professional medical, psychological, psychiatric, legal, or financial advice.

The concepts discussed, including nervous-system regulation, trauma-related patterns, communication dynamics, and the Mirror-Linguistic Hypothesis, are presented as a framework for reflection and exploration. They are not presented as clinical diagnoses, treatment protocols, or guarantees of outcome. Readers should not use this book to self-diagnose, to discontinue or modify prescribed treatment, or to delay seeking professional help.

If you are experiencing mental health distress, persistent anxiety or depression, intrusive thoughts, trauma symptoms, suicidal ideation, or any condition that affects your safety or daily functioning, please seek support from a qualified healthcare professional. If you believe you may be at immediate risk of harm to yourself or others, contact emergency services or your local crisis support provider right away.

Any references to research, theory, or physiology are included to support discussion and should be interpreted within the limits of this book's scope. The author is not providing medical or clinical services, and no professional relationship is created by reading this book.

To the fullest extent permitted by law, the author and publisher disclaim liability for any loss, injury, or damages arising from the use of, or reliance upon, the information in this book. You are solely responsible for how you interpret and apply the material.

Copyright

www.ingramcontent.com/pod-product-compliance
Lightning Source LLC
Chambersburg PA
CBHW071506140726
47997CB00005B/1880